PENGUIN BOOKS

ON THE PERIMETER

Caroline Blackwood was born and raised in Ulster. The widow of the poet Robert Lowell, she now lives in London, England, with her three children. Her novels include *Corrigan* (Viking), *Great Granny Webster*, which was a runner-up for England's prestigious Booker Prize, *The Stepdaughter*, and *The Fate of Mary Rose*, and she has published a collection of short stories, *Good Night Sweet Ladies*. She is at work on a new novel and on a memoir of Robert Lowell.

Books by Caroline Blackwood

For All That I Found There
The Stepdaughter
Great Granny Webster
The Fate of Mary Rose
Good Night Sweet Ladies

On the Perimeter

CAROLINE BLACKWOOD

Penguin Books

PENGUIN BOOKS

Viking Penguin Inc., 40 West 23rd Street,
New York, New York 10010, U.S.A.
Penguin Books Ltd, Harmondsworth,
Middlesex, England
Penguin Books Australia Ltd, Ringwood,
Victoria, Australia
Penguin Books Canada Limited, 2801 John Street,
Markham, Ontario, Canada L3R 1B4
Penguin Books (N.Z.) Ltd, 182–190 Wairau Road,
Auckland 10, New Zealand

First published in Great Britain by William Heinemann Ltd. 1984
First published in the United States of America
with an Afterword by Penguin Books 1985

Published simultaneously in Canada

Library of Congress Cataloging in Publication Data
Blackwood, Caroline.
On the perimeter.
1. Women and peace. 2. Antinuclear movement—Great
Britain. I. Title.
JX1965.B57   1985   327.1'72'088042   85-11996
ISBN 0 14 00.8322 7

Map by Paul Pugliese
Printed in the United States of America by
R. R. Donnelley & Sons Company, Harrisonburg, Virginia
Set in Baskerville

To Evgenia, Ivana and Sheridan

Perimeter: the boundary of a
fortified position; the outer
edge of any area.

Chambers's Students' Dictionary

I first went to the nuclear protest camps at Greenham Common in March 1984. An American magazine had asked me to write an article on the defeat of the Women's British Peace Movement.

The council of Newbury, the town that is nearest to the base, had just issued an eviction order against the women and they were expected to be cleared from their entrenched two-and-a-half year position on the perimeter fence that encircles the Cruise missile.

I was very curious to meet the Greenham women, for the press had decorated them with such loathsome and frightening adjectives, they had been made to sound almost mythical in their horror. They'd been described as 'belligerent harpies', 'a bunch of smelly lesbians', as 'ragtag and bobtail', and 'the screaming destructive witches of Greenham'.

The charges I had heard issued against them varied in their seriousness. They'd been described as 'a lot of silly women with nothing better to do', a merely contemptuous description. They'd been accused of being 'sex starved', which sounded a lot more deadly because it made them sound so dangerous. They were also described as being in the pay of the Soviet Union, and it was said that many of them were Russian spies.

The Greenham women had been adorned with such a wealth of unflattering descriptions, it made one start to ask dizzying questions. Was it worse to be 'sex starved' or to be in the pay of the Soviet Union?

I found the charge that the Greenham women lived like dogs and that they were smearing Newbury with their excrement almost the most chilling one, although it had less grave political connotations.

The claim of Auberon Waugh that the Greenham women smelt of 'fish paste and bad oysters' also haunted me for it had such distressing sexual associations. I wondered how much time he had spent with them. I didn't think that he lived near Greenham Common, but knew I could be very wrong about that. He could always have passed through Newbury and been asphyxiated by the stench that was emanating from the peace camps.

As these women had been attributed with almost every conceivable unsavoury characteristic, I had become very curious to see why they aroused such violent hatred and to discover how evil-smelling and odious the Greenham women could be.

When I arrived at the missile base, I found that nothing had prepared me for the desolation of the camps the women inhabited. I had visualized camps that looked like the camps of boy scouts, but I discovered nothing of the kind.

At first sight, the camps of the Greenham women looked like derelict piles of refuse that had been allowed to collect on the side of the road. The 'benders' they inhabited were like crazy little igloos made of polythene. As tents and caravans had been forbidden by the local council, they had erected these small and eccentric dwellings by draping a sheet of plastic over bending boughs which they had pegged into the mud. Some of the benders were not more than two feet off the ground and had to be entered on all fours. It was astonishing to see a grey-haired woman going into her bender with the scuttling movements of a rabbit vanishing into its burrow.

All the gates of the base where Greenham women were keeping their vigil of protest had been given the names of the colours of the rainbow. There was Blue Gate, Indigo, Violet, Yellow, etc. These romantic and delicate names were ironically inappropriate. Nothing could be grimmer and less beautiful than these police-guarded gates which cut into the menacing grey of the steel perimeter fence with its nine-mile circumference and its concentration-camp coils of barbed wire.

Nothing could look less beautiful than the Cruise missile base itself, with its vast expanse of concrete, its hideous military buildings and vehicles and the warheads nestling in the silos. Within the perimeter fence, the Americans had certainly created Lowell's 'unforgivable landscape'. Looking into the base, I felt chilled by the thought that Russian missiles were trained on to the very spot where I was standing and I started to understand the fear that had driven these women to this ominous fence to protest against the lethal weapons which they believe are placing humanity on the perimeter of extinction.

The women's camps were squeezed up on the muddy verge of the road which encircles the base, and the multi-coloured plastic of their benders made a colourful and defiant contrast to the menacing grey of the huge perimeter fence on which they had taken their miserable position.

I had not realized that the women's protest camps were so vulnerably situated. They were sandwiched between two hostile territories inhabited by powerful groups who loathed them for different reasons. On one side, they had the grey teeming world of the Cruise missile base with its values of the police and the military. On the other side, they had the prosperous world of Newbury with its English gardens and thoroughbreds and its values of the wealthy shopkeeper, and the racehorse owner. I soon discovered that both these worlds had an obsessive horror of the peace women.

In the town of Newbury, they were spoken of with revulsion and some kind of terror. 'We get them up *here*!' a shopkeeper told me in a shocked whisper.

Newbury is only about three miles away from the Cruise missile, but with its red-brick period houses, its W.H. Smith and Sainsbury's and its respectable bustling streets full of shoppers, it seemed light years away from the peace camps. When I was told that they'd 'got them up here', the camps were made to sound like invisible sewers and the shopkeeper could have been speaking of rats.

3

Two paratroopers were standing behind the first women's camp that I visited. They were only separated from the benders by the barbed wire of the great fence and they looked caged, like ferocious animals as they glared at the benders with an expression of venomous hatred that ironically was mingled with fear, as if they felt that it was the women who had the dangerous weapons.

There seemed to be only one woman at Blue Gate that day. She was completely ignoring the anger of the paratroopers and the military police who were so near to her that she could have shaken hands with them. While they paced and champed behind the fence making dark silhouettes of power against the vast grey expanse of the base that they were defending, she just sat there in her freezing little mockery of a 'living-room' which was nothing more than a flimsy piece of plastic that had been draped like a roof over four supporting branches. She was doing a bit of knitting. She only got up to put the kettle on her camp-fire in order to make a cup of tea. I wondered what caused the military to display such hatred towards her for it seemed quite inappropriate to the situation.

I felt frightened as I went to speak to the peace woman. I was frightened to walk past the police and the paratroopers as they stamped with fury and disapproval. It seemed a gratuitously foolish act to walk past them as though I was walking into the front lines of the enemy. They had such a nasty yellow-eyed expression, I felt they might easily shoot me. They made it all too plain that they considered it a criminal offence for any woman to speak to a 'Greenham woman'. It was as if they saw the peace campers as leprous and felt that anyone who had any contact with them might spread the contagion throughout the community, and for this reason would be better exterminated.

I had to remind myself that it was not a crime for a British citizen to speak to another on an English common. I had to remind myself that I was on an English common, for Greenham Common had been so desecrated by the missile base that it had all the grisly melancholy of a modern battle-field on which many people had died.

I had to remind myself that technically these police and paratroopers were mine, in the sense that my taxes paid them to protect me. They were also the paratroopers and police of the English woman making tea in the polythene tent. But that seemed truly unbelievable.

From my first entrance into one of the peace camps, I started to realize that the civic rights of the individual were seen as obsolete on Greenham Common. It was as if everyone in the territory surrounding the Cruise missile saw himself as part of a community engaged in a dangerous war. If the war was a little unbalanced – a tiny group of women fighting the whole might of the military – that did not change the wartime thinking. All rules could be changed to suit any emergency; martial law could be imposed at any given moment.

As I went into the camp at Blue Gate, I was not only frightened of the soldiers who were guarding it. I was frightened of the peace woman, who, having made her tea, had resumed her knitting.

The ugly newspaper descriptions of the Greenham women had stirred up ridiculous images in my unconscious. I saw that she was quite old, that she had grey hair. If she was a Greenham witch, I hated the idea that she might get up and scream at me. If she was as destructive as I'd been told, she might give me a vicious stab with her knitting needles. But above all, I dreaded that she might suddenly behave like a dog and defecate.

Not surprisingly, the woman who introduced herself as Pat did none of these things. She was very friendly and dignified and she offered me the best seat by her fire which made me feel uneasy because it soon turned out she'd been sitting in this awful bender for a year and I'd only dropped in on her frightful conditions in the condescending role of the reporter.

It was bitterly cold in the plastic structure she had made into her living-room. There were no chairs so one had to perch on logs and the planks of a packing-case to get near the fire.

'Are you all alone?' I asked her feebly.

5

I'd expected to find many Greenham women in the camps and it was disturbing to discover only one elderly woman sitting all by herself in this freezing camp on the side of the road.

'No, I'm not alone. Mary is here. But she's been in great pain all night. She's had a horrible migraine. So I've persuaded her to go and lie down.'

She waved her hand at a nearby plastic bender, so low on the ground that it looked like a stray piece of mud-splattered polythene that had been blown on to the side of the road by an accidental gust of wind.

At Blue Gate, as later at all the other gates, I was constantly astonished that the sheets of polythene lying scattered on the ground all around the fire that was the centre of the camp, actually contained living human beings. A foot would suddenly move and it made one jump.

Mary's bender was a particularly miserable one and it looked like the very worst place in which to lie down to try and fight off a migraine. She was lying in very thick mud. She looked like a corpse, over which a sheet had been thrown for the purposes of preserving its human decency.

Pat was a gentle and intelligent woman. She was sensibly dressed for the awful conditions her conscience had forced her to live in. She was wearing trousers and heavy boots and a bulky jacket.

Her face was blue from the cold. She looked exhausted. The floor of her Blue Gate 'living-room' was mud. She had mud on her boots, but that was hardly surprising. Did the mud make her dirty? In a sense, it did. There was no water at Blue Gate except for the water that was carried to the camp in white plastic containers. The containers certainly looked unaesthetic and added to the camp's chaotic appearance. The piles of wood for the fire also looked messy. So did the plastic cups and the saucepans which were all on the ground because the camp had no kitchen.

'You must be quite lonely here,' I said to Pat, wishing immediately that I hadn't said something so stupid. She must see me as an imbecile stating the obvious. Of course it must be desperately lonely for this woman to be sitting hour after hour all by herself on the roadside with the rain beating down on the polythene roof of her bender and the wind blowing out her fire, and only the inhuman perimeter fence and the loathing of the paratroopers for company.

Pat said that she was indeed very lonely. 'They've got almost all our women in Holloway.'

I asked her why they had been imprisoned. Apparently it was for breaking into the base. I was astonished that it was so easy to break into such a grim and huge military installation. I'd imagined that a weapon as important as the Cruise missile would have had very tight security. But Pat said that the women broke in almost every night – that they did so in order to point out that this lethal weapon on which so much money had been spent was pathetically ill-defended. She insisted that they did no harm once they got within the base and the control tower. The worst they might do was to paint a peace symbol on a military vehicle. They only broke in to make the public aware that it was highly dangerous to keep such a deadly foreign weapon on English soil.

'The young girls on the camps really love their symbols,' she said. 'You know, they weave all these webs. They hold mirrors up to the base so as to make it reflect its own evil – I'm a bit old for all that.'

She said that she had moved to the camps because her conscience forced her to live beside the missile. She felt someone had to make a protest and draw public attention to the dangers of turning England into a Russian target.

'If no one makes any fuss, there will be a catastrophe and the world is so beautiful I really can't bear it.'

Pat told me that she was a grandmother and that in one sense she'd joined the camps for the sake of her children and grandchildren. Earlier this morning she had gone into the woods to collect sticks and she'd come across a fawn. She knew that I might find her sentimental, but she'd imagined him with radiation burns and she'd found the idea unspeakable.

Later I discovered that almost all the women of Greenham

were passionate animal lovers and that there were even a few who had condemned themselves to the subhuman conditions of the camps on behalf of the moles, the flowers, the trees. As these women saw it, the animals and birds and fishes were much more innocent and worthy of sacrifice than humanity for they had not invented the destructive weapons that could make the planet uninhabitable. These pro-earth women saw human beings as so stupid and suicidal that they felt there was hardly any point making any protest against the destruction they were trying to wreak on themselves. But they were still prepared to make a protest on behalf of the planet, and if they failed and were blown up and perished in torment in a nuclear disaster they still felt they would die happier knowing that their consciences were clear, that they'd done all in their feeble power to avert the cataclysmic tragedy.

Pat kept apologizing for the smoke from her fire which was streaming into our eyes as we huddled round it in order to avoid frost-bite. We both looked as if we were in floods of tears. In the mornings all the Greeham women had scarlet eyes and looked as if they had spent the whole night crying.

'I suppose we will all get cancer of the eye.' Pat gave a shrug. She spoke with the curious dead-pan resignation that I soon found was very typical of all the women in the peace camps. They took everything that happened to them in their stride. The hooligan youths from Newbury came down in the night and poured pigs' blood and maggots and excrement all over them. Red-hot pokers were shoved through their polythene benders in order to terrify them. The bushes near their camps were set on fire.

They had to put up with every kind of insult from the soldiers and the press, but nothing seemed able to ruffle the odd calm that came from the knowledge that they were obeying their consciences. They felt that they *had* to keep up their protest. It was a spiritual position and words could not give it expression.

As compared with the medical effects of the nuclear holocaust that Pat saw as impending, unless her protest was listened to, cancer of the eye was quite a minor ailment.

Pigs' blood and excrement could all be wiped off even though the women found it ghastly to have to clean it off with freezing water on a winter's morning. All the degradations that they suffered paled beside the potential human suffering that could be created by the warheads.

In real life, as opposed to life at Greenham in which everything seemed unreal, Pat was a geriatric nurse. I asked her if her children approved of her having abandoned her profession and joined the peace camps. Her two daughters were apparently embarrassed by what she was doing. They disliked having a mother who had taken a disreputable position in which she lived like a beggar on the side of the road. It was easy to imagine two respectable daughters finding Pat's self-imposed and unenviable situation very difficult to come to terms with.

'But my son supports what I am doing.' She smiled, obviously finding it ironic that it should be the male of her family who gave support to a peace movement from which men were excluded.

'My son always comes down and visits me here and he brings me things,' Pat said.

I felt that it must be very strange and disturbing for the son when he had to leave her, knowing that he was going back to a warm bed while his mother was going to sleep out in the bitter cold, in all the squalor of the camp.

'And my grandchildren admire me for doing this.' Pat made a pendulum gesture with her hand that signified the swinging attitudes of each generation.

'Isn't it funny how things go in families?'

She put on a kettle to make us tea. I soon found that in the camps it was a fantastic event whenever anyone made a cup of tea. Everyone watched the woman who made it as if they were watching a riveting theatrical performance. This was because the hours dragged so unbearably. There was just this deadly endless sitting with everyone's back aching from the lack of support that damp logs provide when they are used as chairs. Every time anyone made a cup of tea or a French toast in a frying-pan, it gave one the exciting feeling that at last something had happened.

The dreariest little domestic act interrupted the terrible monotony and the feeling of *Waiting for Godot*. In the camps there were only hours stretching out into a future as grey as the fence of the missile base. There would be days, and the days would be nothing but boring hours, of sitting. There would be nights with hours that would be exactly the same, except they would seem longer because the sitting would take place in the dark, and the cold would become much more extreme and the night hours would bring many more terrors of sudden attack from hostile forces, such as the vigilantes from Newbury.

'How do you get food here?' I asked. I couldn't see how Pat got anything here, for her camp seemed to be in the back of nowhere. And yet just across the road there was a prosperous looking red-brick stockbroker-type house with mullioned windows and a two-car garage and although it was so near, it seemed miles away for it looked immensely opulent – as if it could go straight into the pages of *Country Life*, and it seemed weird that this house which represented respectability and wealth should be situated on the very perimeter of Pat's self-chosen poverty. Everything was right on top of everything else at Greenham Common, the peace women were right on top of the military, and the expensive houses and the Newbury golf-club and the race-course were right on top of the peace camps.

Although everything geographically was lying hugger-mugger, nothing connected between the groups. All their varying ideals created an immeasurable distance between the different factions.

Pat shrugged when I asked her how she got any food, that resigned and mysterious Buddhist monk shrug. They lived on the contributions of supporters. People brought them things. She didn't appear to feel that food was very important. She hardly seemed to regard it as a basic need. If it came, it came. If it didn't come, they simply did without. She saw firewood and candles as the most essential items in the peace women's battle for survival. She said that it was awful when they ran out of candles and firewood at night.

'Some of the pop stars send us hampers,' she told me. 'We hear about them, but they don't often reach us. They won't deliver parcels here. It's not a proper address. I don't know what happens to the hampers. Maybe they eat them in the Newbury post office!'

She was joking, but it was a curious picture. The well-fed postal workers of Newbury swigging down the champagne and eating the foie gras that had been provided by Paul McCartney.

She asked me if I was going back to London. If I ran into anyone there who planned to send them a parcel, could I please ask them not to send one. Only postal orders addressed to the Main Gate were valuable. She hated people to waste their money.

This request made me realize how cut-off some of the Greenham women were. They felt they could only send messages to the outside world by word of mouth. They were in touch only with the other camps round the base.

'Are you soon being evicted?' I asked her.

Again she shrugged. 'Oh, yes. They are going to evict us quite soon.' She pointed apologetically to the disordered appearance of the camp. 'We used to keep things much tidier. But now that we've heard that there's an eviction order and we are only really waiting for the bailiffs, there just doesn't seem much point in trying to keep the camp neat. We know that they will throw our things all over the place and rip up the benders and make such a mess of it that we feel too exhausted to try and spruce it up. It just seems much too pointless.'

It certainly did seem pointless. If the camp was going to be destroyed within the week, it was obviously totally futile for her to waste her energies doing 'housework'.

'Where will you go when you are evicted?'

She shrugged again. She didn't know. But she wasn't going to leave the base – that was all that she knew.

I felt only astonishment when she told me this. How could this grey-haired sensible grandmother feel so deeply that it was imperative that she remained beside the gates of the base?

How could she think that her presence there would be effective in bringing about the international disarmament she dreamed of? The base looked gigantic. It contained the might of the most powerful country in the world. Unimaginable sums of money had gone into that base. How could this woman, with her plastic cup and bender, believe that anything could move that base except an enemy missile?

She seemed to guess what I was thinking. 'Oh, yes,' she said. 'Of course I get moods when I wonder what the hell I am doing here. We all get moods like that. When the women get sent to prison they feel they are being given a rest. Holloway is a much better place to be than here. At least you have a roof and water and regular food. Holloway is a heavenly holiday after you've been at Greenham.'

I felt it must be an unusual position for the magistrates in the courts at Newbury as they meted out their daily punishments to women who saw these punishments as free trips to luxurious living.

'When I get those moods they never last very long,' Pat said. 'I think of the grandchildren and I know I have no choice. I know I *have* to be here and I just get on with it. I know I couldn't sleep well in my old age if I didn't do this.'

Mary suddenly rose up out of her low bender like Lazarus rising from the dead. She looked very young to me, about eighteen. Many of the 'Greenham women' looked so young that I found it impossible to remember to call them 'women' and I kept referring to them as girls. I knew this was a political error for the peace women only wish to be known as 'women' and they feel that calling them 'girls' is an insult, like referring to a black man as a 'nigger'. But I kept making this mistake, and I was relieved to notice that Pat kept making it too. The 'women' would correct us, but only as a joke. They saw that it was hopeless for us to remember to call them something which we felt was ridiculously inaccurate.

Mary looked desperately unwell. Her face was pinched with pain and she was blue with cold. Her sweater was soaking wet from lying on the ground and she took it off and hung it on a washing-line and put on another one which only looked half dried out from the feeble heat that was being given out by the fire. The drying of clothes was an endless problem in the camps. Even when it wasn't raining the fires never provided enough heat to dry anything very satisfactorily. The women would wrap themselves in blankets so that their wet clothes created damp heat, but then the blankets themselves got wet and all their coverings were sodden.

Pat asked Mary how she felt. Not surprisingly Mary's 'rest' under the sheet of polythene had not helped her at all. Her migraine was apparently worse than ever. Pat told her that she was sorry and she put on the kettle to make her some tea. Making someone tea was the remedy for all ills within the camps. Women became upset after they'd received some vicious insult from the military – they became agitated after they'd been into Newbury and people in the streets had spat at them. They suffered from every kind of physical ailment. They received bad news from home, including the news of deaths within their families. The response to these varying afflictions was identically the same. Someone put their arm round them while someone else made them a cup of tea. The staple fare of the peace camps was 'tea and sympathy', which was the only warmth they were able to provide.

'Do you get very bored here?' I asked Pat and Mary.

'It's dead boring,' Mary said.

Pat didn't find it so boring. She read, she knitted, she did a little painting. She thought it was much worse for the young ones, it was more boring for them because there were more things they'd prefer to be doing.

'I really admire them,' she said.

I told Pat that I was writing an article about the peace camps and she was neither interested nor scornful. She said that many people had written about the Greenham women, that they were mostly lies and she felt it was a waste of time to read them. I could understand that it would be rather futile for Pat to sit on Greenham Common reading lies about the Greenham women. Like many other peace women to whom I spoke later, Pat seemed to be both far above and far below the media. She was above it in the sense that she had total contempt for it. She had the sophisticated belief that it was completely corrupt, that it manipulated public opinion by censoring and slanting every item of news that it reported. She was below it and was unsophisticated in the sense that she had as little connection with any branch of the media as a bird or bee.

She recognized that it had power, but its power was far too remote from her to allow her to nurse any belief that it could ever be of any help to the cause which had brought her to Blue Gate.

'I am so tired,' Pat said. 'We had such an awful night with the soldiers. They abused us all night. They just wouldn't stop. It was sexual, of course. It's always sexual.'

Apparently many of the soldiers were under the impression that all the peace women were only camping round the base because they wanted to sleep with them. This was such a vain and deluded assumption, it was comic. Never had any group of men seemed less sexually desirable than the defenders of the Cruise missile when seen from the peace camps.

Within their given role on the perimeter they often hardly seemed like men, they seemed more like dangerous beasts. They were figures to be feared for their cruelty, but this gave them no erotic charisma. The foulness of their language as they shouted at the peace women befouled *them* rather than the women. They seemed besplattered with their own oaths and soiled by their own sordid fantasies.

What is the matter with these soldiers, I wondered when I later heard them bellowing their horrible obscenities. The peace women seem to have deranged them. They were probably perfectly sympathetic as individuals. Presumably they wouldn't carry on like dirty-minded schoolboys at home. Yet the peace women brought out everything that was sadistic and infantile in these men. The sex war that was raging on the perimeter was a very ugly and cruel one.

'Why do they hate you so much?' I asked Pat. She said that

the soldiers had been told that they wouldn't have to stand there guarding the base if it wasn't for the Greenham women.

The lives of the soldiers certainly seemed to be dismal. Their job was much more 'dead boring' than that of the peace women. They too were out in the cold and the rain hour after hour. But they had none of the jokes and the camaraderie that alleviated the tedium of the peace camps. People were not arriving from all over England to show their support for them. No one ever brought them gifts like they brought the peace women.

'But how can the soldiers be so stupid as to think that they only have to guard the base because of the peace women?' I asked Pat. I couldn't understand how the military could imagine that they could have nuclear warheads just sitting there in the silos with no one guarding them.

She gave her usual shrug. 'A lot of soldiers are not very bright,' she said. 'They believe what they are told. Maybe that's part of being a soldier.'

She told me that the regiments and the individual soldiers varied and that some of the men were much kinder to the peace women than others. She said that the Coldstreams were usually very nice men and they seemed highly intelligent. I found it fascinating to learn that in the peculiar situation existing on the missile base, the Coldstreams were living up to their shining tradition of discipline and chivalry.

Pat told me that the Greenham women were prepared to damage military property, but they would never do anything to hurt the soldiers. 'We have a horror of violence so we will never do anything to hurt a person.'

She said that last Christmas when they had sent balloons up into the air as a gesture of protest, they had thought of putting pieces of tin-foil in them because they wanted the public to know that just a few bits of tin-foil could disrupt the entire radar system of the missile base, but although they wanted to make their point that nuclear weapons did not protect the lives of British citizens, but endangered them because they brought such a risk of the catastrophic accident, they had sent up the balloons without any tin-foil.

'We could have made some plane crash,' Pat said. 'That would have been a really wicked thing to do. We do not believe in being irresponsible.'

Of all the awful things that the Greenham women had been accused of, Pat most objected to the charge that they had whipped police horses with strands of barbed wire. She said that although this was the soiling rumour that was spread about them, no woman to her knowledge had ever been arrested on such a charge. She would like to know why the police had been so curiously restrained in the face of such criminal provocation. If the police had made arrests on this particular charge, the Greenham women would have all supported them.

'The whole rumour is so idiotic,' Pat said. 'Can you imagine a pacifist woman attacking an animal? And the rumour makes the police look like numbskulls. They make no arrests when their horses are brutalized. Yet they make arrests when someone snips the perimeter wire ...'

She couldn't understand why the press made such a fuss about the lesbians who were on the camps.

'Surely, nowadays, people know that lesbians exist. Why make such a big thing about it? Think how many gays they have in the army.'

I asked her why the Greenham women had decided to exclude men from their camps. She said that she knew that they were criticized for this, and people felt that it was a great mistake that they had rejected such a huge body of support. She still felt that the protest would have fizzled out if they had allowed men on the camps. Men always wanted to create a hierarchy and the Greenham women had none. There was no one in charge at the camps. No one ever told anyone else to do anything. If no one felt like cooking, no one cooked. Eventually someone would feel like doing it.

Pat believed that men would find the absence of leadership on the camps intolerable. She thought that if the women had accepted the male idea that someone *must* be in charge they would never have survived the 'ambush of the winter'. If they'd established a system in which orders had to be obeyed, everyone would have very soon got fed up and gone home. Their system only worked because none of the women ever felt that they were *meant* to do anything. Anything they did for the community, such as gathering wood, cooking, and washing up in cold water, was entirely voluntary.

'Whenever you read that "a spokeswoman for the Greenham women said" – you know it's bogus,' Pat told me. 'We don't have a spokeswoman on the Common. Or rather we are all spokeswomen.'

She felt that at heart, most men worshipped weapons, force, and power, and it was difficult for them to understand why many women loathed and feared these particular manifestations of masculinity.

She accepted that many women also supported the male ethic and were even more weapon-worshipping than their fathers and husbands. Such women would obviously loathe the whole idea of the camps. She realized that there were also many men who were in complete sympathy with the peace women and would fit in very well at Greenham Common, but it had seemed impossible to make an exclusive selection. I could understand that the peace women couldn't really make their male supporters do an oral and written examination before they were considered suitable material for these wretched camps. It would be absurd if they had to apply like students struggling for admission to a university.

Pat made the emphatic point that it never seemed to occur to the men who objected to being excluded from the Greenham Common camps that they could easily form their own. If they felt so strongly about the threat of nuclear destruction, there was nothing to stop them setting up their own protest groups. She suspected they didn't feel as strongly as they pretended because they had less identification with the fate and the future of their children and their grandchildren. She also felt, with many other Greenham women, that if they'd had men on their camps the military and the police and the hooligan youths from Newbury would have used much more violence in trying to quell the protest. Women tended to be more accustomed to derision and insult, they were more conditioned to ignoring provocation. She thought that many males would find it insufferably emasculating to be asked to behave with the passivity that was required on the camps. They would feel their non-violent role was cowardly and despicable if they had to sit around and listen to the brutal youths from Newbury as they drove past the camps screaming maniacal abuse at the women.

As we talked, jockeys kept riding past along the road that encircled the base. Their beautiful rippling thoroughbred horses clopped along on the tarmac as if Greenham Common was still a suitable place to exercise. The short-stirruped riders deliberately avoided casting even a 'cold eye' on the camp at Blue Gate, as if they believed that if they resolutely refused to look at it, it would somehow magically vanish. They behaved in the same way with the military and the police who were guarding the gateway of the base. The jockeys simply refused to look at them. They seemed to view them with a horror equal to that with which they clearly viewed the Greenham women. Both had wrecked the calm and beauty of an English common. They rode by as if they were riding in the past on springy green turf, and their averted eyes expressed their desire to avoid any confrontation with the menacing by-products of modernity.

Pat said that the women had been evicted before and she was certain they would survive the imminent evictions.

In the past, the Newbury council had completely demolished the camp that was outside the Main Gate and covered the land with piles of huge boulders. This militant procedure had been euphemistically described as 'landscaping'. The women had not been defeated. They had gone right back and put up their benders on top of all the rocks. As the months had gone by, they had slowly cleared them away. Their role in regard to the boulders sounded like that of Sisyphus.

She said that in the past the bailiffs had been very kind to the peace women. They had torn down their benders because they had their living to earn and they were paid to do so by the Council. But then later when they were 'off duty' they had helped to rebuild them.

It was curious to hear that the bailiffs, those figures who traditionally have always been loathed and feared, should have turned out to have behaved like ministering angels to the peace women.

Pat said that the bailiffs didn't enjoy their job. They had wives and mothers and sisters and they felt it was ignoble to tear the only shelter that a woman had from over her head. They were even more embarrassed doing it to the older women, and they particularly hated destroying the benders when it was raining.

'You can see we don't have much,' Pat said, pointing round the camp. 'They don't like taking our belongings and throwing them into the "scruncher" and pulping them. You always see that in their faces.'

Pat certainly didn't seem to have very much on her camp, a few plastic cups, and a frying-pan, and the all important blackened kettle. 'From them that have *not* shall be taken away. Yea, even that which he hath.' The bailiffs might well feel uneasy as they carried out their biblical instructions.

'The Quakers and the bailiffs have been very good to us,' Pat said. This seemed to me an unlikely alliance of two groups whom I would have expected to have many profound ideological differences.

As I talked to Pat, it seemed absurd to think that this courageous and dignified nurse was seen as a 'destructive dirty harpy' in the public imagination. The same qualities of patience and altruism that had given her the strength to devote her life to alleviating the sufferings of the very old with their unhopeful situation, their lack of glamour, and their incontinence and senile dementia, had sunk her down in the mud on Greenham Common.

I told Pat that I was going to leave and drive round the other camps to see how they were faring in the face of their imminent eviction. I felt upset leaving her all alone with only Mary, who was speechless from the pain of her migraine and very poor company indeed. But Pat obviously wanted me to go and see whether the other camps had been destroyed. The peace women felt so separated from each other by the size of the vast perimeter fence and their lack of transport that they worried continually about the welfare of the women in the other camps, just as mothers worry neurotically about absent children.

'I could use the car and go into Newbury. I could bring you back food, pain-killers for Mary's migraine. I could bring you back anything – if you'd only give me a list,' I said to her.

Neither Pat nor Mary wanted me to go into Newbury to buy anything for them. Mary very often had migraines – she always got over them in the end. Pain-killers never much helped her. They said that there was very little that was *not* needed at Blue Gate. They desperately required Fairy Liquid and candles. But there was no point in anyone bringing them any of these items. It was just a waste of time. If the Fairy Liquid and the candles were going to be thrown into the 'scruncher' the next day, it seemed stupid to waste money.

2

At Green Gate, I saw my first web. It was tiny and made of blue wool and attached to the branch of a tree. This was what the young girls apparently loved. It had been very cleverly woven, but it still seemed a bad peace symbol. Many people have a terrible fear of spiders. Webs are sticky and you get caught in them. Once caught in a web, metaphorically you die. The peace women saw the web as a symbol of strength. Although composed of feeble strands, each added strand adds strength to the web. The explanation was all right, but as few people knew it, the web still seemed a very unfortunate peace sign.

The symbol of the snake, which was also beloved of the young girls on Greenham Common, disturbed me too. Why had they chosen such a stupidly frightening and poisonous symbol? Again, the snake was a deeply feared creature. It didn't seem to have very much to do with either peace or women.

The snake, like the web, turned out to be a little better than it seemed, once it was explained. The snake sheds its skin and survives. It still seemed a great mistake when the peace women painted snakes on army trucks. The military couldn't be expected to understand the subtle symbolism. In Newbury, the webs and the snakes were known as the graffiti of the Greenham Common women. The word graffiti had the usual bad lavatory associations that were always attributed to the peace women.

Pat had told me that Green Gate was the camp of the intellectuals. She'd made it sound like All Souls, but it wasn't like that at all. There was no exquisite wine or port and the women were too exhausted and cold to make brilliant John Sparrow donnish conversation.

It was not very near the perimeter. It was pushed off to the side in a depressing patch of scrubby woods. It was quite far from the action. Only in its cut-off position did it seem to represent the typical plight of the intellectuals.

There were quite a lot of women at Green Gate. Their conditions were just as bad as those of Mary and Pat. The woods made their camp seem darker and damper than Blue Gate. They had a very bad fire and no chairs. They told me that their 'cuisine' was not their strongest point. They had one hot meal a day – it was nearly always rice. Sometimes people brought them something exciting like a pimento and they threw it into the pot and pretended they were having French cooking.

There was no feeling of 'Make Love, not War' at Green Gate, nor was there at any of the other camps for that matter. There was none of the festive feeling of the peace demonstrations of the 1960s. It was extremely grim. It lacked any of the carefree feeling of the 'Demo' outing for the day. This was a long drawn-out battle for sheer survival. This was a self-inflicted misery that had already been prolonged – a misery that would continue into a future that had no definable limit.

How long will these women sit here in the freezing cold, I wondered? How do they bear the rain, and the snow? How do they bear the lack of any washing facilities? How do they bear the boredom of all this ghastly sitting?

As I went from camp to camp, from Blue to Green, to Indigo, to Turquoise, I found it difficult to decide which would be the most terrible of all these ill-named rainbow gates to live in.

Yellow Gate, known as Main Gate, was the only one that had a tap with running water. But it had other horrible disadvantages. It had all the noise of the enormous military juggernauts and the motor bikes and the jeeps and the other vehicles that streamed in and out of the base. Orange Gate had less traffic noise, but the women who lived there were more squeezed up against the perimeter fence and were therefore nearer to the soldiers who could keep them awake all night with the terrible sexual taunting. The soldiers had the energy to abuse and jeer at the women all through the night hours because they were warmed by their braziers and when they changed guard they could go and get some sleep. A new lot of paratroopers could then take over, feeling fresh for the sexual verbal attack. The women felt obliged to stay at their icy-cold posts and could not take it in shifts as they endured the onslaught.

They were literally frozen to the spot where they had made the ideological promise to alert the nation of the exact time when the warheads would leave the base and travel through the English countryside to the launching pads.

The Greenham women believed that it was highly dangerous for the warheads to go travelling through the English countryside – even on military practice manoeuvres. The Russian satellite cameras would photograph the missile carriers as they left the base. They would have no way of knowing whether the carriers were only doing a practice run. They might think the warheads were being deployed for a First Strike and react with hysteria – thinking their country was under a lethal threat.

The women also believed that military practice manoeuvres were dangerous on another level. The fifty-foot carriers were suited to American highways, but most unsuited to English roads. British drivers of these huge vehicles would not be accustomed to the left-hand drive. The drivers would be under great stress and highly nervous from the responsibility of transporting their deadly cargo. All this increased the risk of an accident in which plutonium could be spilled and poison the environment.

It was because the women felt obliged to keep a vigil on all the gates of the base so that the lives of British civilians could never be put in danger without their knowledge, that their camps were so excruciatingly uncomfortable. Guerrillas and fleeing war victims and other such groups who form camps for their survival try to find sites that have certain features that make them suitable for camping. They try to select places where there is water and shelter. But the women had not got this choice. Their position as witnesses forced them to stay at the gates where many of the sites were waterless and exposed and disastrously situated. They combined all the discomforts of the wilderness with many of the horrors of civilization.

At Green Gate I remembered that I'd been told that the women only joined the camps because they had nothing better to do and this accusation seemed grotesque. Almost anything seemed preferable to do than sitting around freezing in the desolation of this awful camp. Many of the women there were teachers, nurses and students. Obviously they would all prefer to be carrying on with their professions.

There was one girl at Green Gate who seemed to be mentally ill. She kept twitching and shaking and she had the haunted unseeing expression of those who are suffering from some profound emotional disturbance.

There was a sudden roar from the perimeter. It sounded like a herd of bulls roaring. It was the first time that I'd heard the soldiers shouting abuse at the women. I was very glad that Green Gate was comparatively removed from the military. But their hatred was conveyed and the hatred was frightening, and it seemed all the more so because the women were out of sight of the soldiers and there was something very eerie about them shouting at women whom they couldn't even see. When the shaking, twitching girl heard the roar of the soldiers, she suddenly started to cry.

'They've been doing that all night,' she sobbed. 'They are trying to send us mad. If you are never allowed to sleep it's meant to send you mad. I think I may be going mad! I think I'm having a breakdown.'

One of the women gathered round the fire went over to the girl and patted her soothingly on the knee like someone patting a dog. 'You are going to be all right,' she said. 'But I think you ought to go and lie down. When things start to get on top of one, I think it's always a good thing to take a nap.'

24

It was perfectly sensible advice. It only seemed incongruous in the circumstances in which it was given. Would the girl really feel that things were 'less on top of her' if she went to lie down under one of the sheets of polythene with a blanket that was wringing wet?

It was probable that this particular girl was far too ill to have anything much better to do than sit in the peace camps. She gave the impression that she would have broken down even in the most comfortable outside-world conditions. It seemed unlikely that her unhappy mental state was caused by the vicissitudes of existence on Greenham Common.

In the outside world she would probably have been put in a mental home. I wondered if she was not just a little better off at Green Gate. She refused to take a nap because she obviously couldn't face the isolation and cold of lying alone in one of the benders, but the women did their best to cheer her up and they took it in turns to pat her, which eventually calmed her down. I wondered if this treatment was not just as effective as drugging her.

She got a lot more attention from the Greenham women than she would get in most hospitals, and she seemed to respond to it. The inevitable cup of tea was made for her and she was offered little pieces of cheese. It was exciting to see her eat it. It seemed a sign that she felt more 'on top of things'.

Just when life seemed intolerably tedious on the peace camps, some small event would occur to divert one. Two very young nuns suddenly came winding through the woods. They were from Cork. They had come over on the ferry and walked all the way from there to Greenham Common. They had brought some raisins for the women. They'd heard that the women needed people to keep vigil on the gates and they'd come to offer to do it. Vigil at Green Gate was a highly unpleasant duty because it meant standing up all night right in front of the soldiers. I wondered how these sheltered little nuns were going to take the sexual insults of the military.

A Dutch woman then arrived at the camp. She was wearing a luxurious fur coat which looked curious in contrast to the average clothes of the peace women with their bulky jackets, their rubber trousers and hefty boots.

At first I felt she was rather courageous in daring to be so conspicuously different. But she wasn't really being all that brave. Her expensive fur coat created little stir even in the uneventfulness of the camps.

One of the most liberating feelings in the eccentric little community that the peace women had created was the realization that no one gave a damn how you looked. You could look hideous, you could look very old, you could look rich or poor or pretty or downright crazy. If your ears were aching from the biting wind you could cover them with a pair of woolly tights and no one would even notice the peculiarity of your head-dress. Appearance simply didn't matter at all on Greenham Common and this relieved an anxiety and pressure that is present all the time in ordinary society, even if one is hardly aware of it. When it was abolished by the tolerant attitude of the peace women, a pointless burden was lifted and the effect was refreshing and pleasant. The Dutch woman sat herself down on a piece of wet cardboard which she first carefully dusted and someone made her the usual cup of tea.

No one seemed to know why anyone had come to the camps. It was just accepted that they had arrived. Women came from all over the world. A lot of Australians and Americans would suddenly turn up. A bus load of women would appear from Spain. Benders had to be made for them. They were always given the best food that was available. I was astonished by the way that the Greenham women managed their very severe problems as hostesses. I knew I could never be so calm if 150 strangers from Sweden turned up without warning at my house and I had to feed them. But the Greenham women somehow managed. They never appeared to be ruffled by any of the impromptu arrivals. Because of the floating in and out nature of the camps it was impossible to gauge how many women were actually protesting at the base at any given moment. There was one solid coterie of permanent Greenham residents, then there were the semi-residents who only camped part-time and also had part-time jobs. Then there were the campers from abroad who came only for a short time in order to make a gesture of support.

Women often hardly knew each other's names on the camps. Sometimes one got to know their first names, but with such a constant influx of women their surnames were impossible to remember. Names hardly seemed to matter on the camps, and neither did the women's ordinary occupations. They were just 'women' and they shared a terror of 'nukes' and that was all they had to unify them.

I was told that there was hardly a profession that was not represented on the camps. 'We have two psychoanalysts living on the base,' a Scottish girl told me. 'We also have a forester. Isn't it funny to think of a forester meeting a psychoanalyst. I'm sure they would never have normally met in their entire lives.'

This was very probably true.

A woman from Yorkshire suddenly joined the group at Green Gate and she kept saying how wonderful it was to be out in the cold. No one who was sitting around agreed with her at all. But she then explained she'd spent the whole morning in the Newbury courthouse, where it had been so hot it had been suffocating. I wondered why the Newbury courthouse was like an inferno, but she never really explained. I still got a powerful image of a magistrate sweltering as he tried case after case of Greenham women.

The new arrival said she'd spent the morning in court giving support to a woman who was accused of cutting the perimeter fence. A soldier had identified her and he had given a lot of long, drawn-out evidence, all of which proved her to be the culprit. The woman had let him give his testimony without making any objection. He was asked which hand he'd seen her use to cut the fence and he swore he'd seen her use her right hand.

When he'd finished, the woman on trial had held up her right hand to the magistrate and showed him that she'd lost her thumb and several fingers in an accident. The magistrate

27

had been discomfited for he'd been just on the point of sentencing her. After seeing her hand, he'd had no choice but to release her.

All the little dramas that took place in the Newbury courtroom were valuable to the peace women because they provided entertainment, something that was desperately lacking in the camps.

Many of the symbolic activities in which the women engaged themselves were employed, ironically, as 'deterrents'. They protected the peace campers from the danger that their will and their determination to remain protesting at the missile might be sapped by insidious boredom.

With brightly coloured wools the women would endlessly darn the steel looped wire of the perimeter fence. All this darning ostensibly represented the humble tasks of womenfolk. Symbolically, the Greenham women seemed only to ask to be allowed life so that they could carry on their useful little modest contribution to humanity's welfare. In symbol, they begged that they be spared from nuclear destruction so that they could still patch up the holes the men had made, and continue to make the male foot rest more comfortably in his shoe.

The peace women's darning of the perimeter was both a black joke and, paradoxically, a light one. Never have I seen such beautiful, meticulous darning. Since the beginning of time, no man has probably ever had his socks and woollens darned with such loving and perfectionist dedication as the Greenham women devoted to darning the perimeter. Huge areas of the hideous fence soon started to look like beautiful tapestries. There were no congested woolly lumps. It all turned into one lovely smooth surface, for they sewed it with such ingenuity and care. But then the military would spot what the women had done and it was the look of rage and horror on their faces that made all this exquisite darning so effective as a boredom 'deterrent'.

The women despised the workings and attitudes of the military mind and they managed to needle it with this ridiculous darning. The soldiers would rush at the patches of darned perimeter like monkeys when they go berserk in their cage. Nothing seemed to anger them like the sight of even the smallest sock-sized darn on the fence that defended the missile.

When the soldiers had finished ripping and tearing off the wool with various sharp instruments, the poor perimeter looked truly terrible. The paratroopers couldn't be bothered to make a really diligent job of removing every strand of wool. That was quite understandable. But the little bits of brightly coloured ruined darns that clung tenaciously to the fence had a sleazy pathos and they looked extremely messy and unpleasant. Why couldn't the military leave things as they were when they were nice? That was the peace women's simple, but also serious symbolic message.

Main Gate, or Yellow Gate, was the largest of the camps. It had a special urban desolation that made it grimmer than the rest of the camps. It was the centre of all the military activity on the missile base. As well as having the usual benders painted with peace signs, the women who camped there had a few old battered ambulances, one of which was occupied by the world-famous baby who had been born on Greenham Common. The ambulances created unpleasant associations, reminding one of accidents and blood.

The military and the Ministry of Defence police who were guarding it displayed the usual loathing of the women. There was a policeman staring at them with such hatred that I couldn't resist asking him what he thought of them.

'Who are the Greenham women?' he asked me. They were all sitting around, only a few yards away from him. He seemed very pleased with his answer. By not recognizing they existed, he appeared to feel he had got rid of them.

I noticed a long patch of newly dug earth lying very near to the fence. Someone had surrounded it with stones and there was such an atmosphere of latent violence at Main Gate I thought it was a grave. It wouldn't have surprised me to learn that some Greenham woman had met with disaster and had ended up buried under the shadow of the perimeter.

An American woman came up to me and told me that the patch was her garden. It seemed a desperate place to garden, with so many military vehicles thundering past. I told the American I'd mistaken her garden for a grave. I hoped that it wouldn't offend her.

'It's a bed of onions,' she said, 'but maybe unconsciously I made it look like a grave. They will trample it any time now.' She gave the same sort of shrug that Pat always gave.

The American woman spent most of the day gardening. She had planted leeks and carrots and tomatoes. 'How can she bear the futility of her occupation,' I wondered. It was the same question that in the light of all the military activity that was going on within the base applied to every peace camper on the Common.

There were lesbians at Main Gate. They had deliberately made themselves look very wild. They created a lot of hostility by their insistence on kissing in public. It obviously maddened the soldiers, and knowing that it had that effect, the lesbians kissed each other much more than was necessary in order to be provocative.

They brought to the camps a confusion of cause. Their right to be lesbian could have been protested anywhere. It was not clear why it had to be so violently demonstrated in front of the Cruise missile. The lesbians were all passionately opposed to nuclear weapons, but I still grew to dread the obligatory embrace into which some plunged whenever they saw a paratrooper or the camera of the media.

Their public kissing was embarrassing because it looked unfelt and exhibitionist. Just because they had seen a television crew it was unlikely that this sight had really made them feel all that sexy. When I visited the Newbury courthouse to watch the trials of various women, some of the Greenham lesbians arrived and sat at the back of the court, and inevitably they started embracing each other. The courtroom is such an un-erotic spot that their behaviour seemed irritatingly inappropriate. It would have been just as disturbing to see a heterosexual couple making love while a trial was proceeding. In the Newbury courtroom, the lesbians seemed determined to over-egg the sexual pudding. Their behaviour seemed aggressive and there was the danger that the hostility it aroused could transfer itself to the peace women who were in the dock and bring them much more punitive sentences.

When the lesbians were alone with all the other women and there was no one around to be shocked, they didn't bother to make much display of their sexual position. They kissed publicly to create outrage, but this seemed short-sighted and silly.

The ferocious image that they liked to present by dressing in deliberately threatening costumes was also self-conscious for they were not in the least ferocious when one talked to them. They looked very frightening from afar and that seemed to give them pleasure but it seemed childish and self-defeating and it gave ammunition to those who hated the position of the Greenham women.

While I was at Main Gate on my first day, the American woman who loved gardening received a letter from her daughter in the United States. She told us that her daughter was begging her to come home, she was apparently in the deepest depression and she cried from the moment that she woke until night fell. She had written to tell her mother that she was consulting a psychiatrist.

'But why doesn't she come over here and join us at Greenham,' all the women immediately asked the American gardener.

'Can you just imagine how often I've asked her to come over,' she said, 'but she won't come. You see, she is very happily married.'

'If she's so happily married, why is she in tears all day long?' someone asked. This seemed a valid point. When the women kept insisting that the American's daughter would be better off at Greenham Common that she'd be with any psychiatrist, at first their contention seemed preposterous. How could a severe depressive be cheered by moving to Main Gate, with all its deprivations and the frightful wind that kept tearing through it with such force that one felt that at any given moment many of the benders would be ripped out of the mud and go flying over the perimeter in the direction of the warheads, which would be symbolically very peculiar?

The benders, in fact, were curiously well-constructed. 'Don't worry, it will be all right,' the women kept assuring me as they saw me wincing as a blast of wind hit the one in which we were all sitting and made the polythene flap like the wild sails of a ship caught in a storm. Like their creators, the benders had a curious resilience. They were built out of such springy branches that they had the ability to sway with the wind like reeds. They were also surprisingly well attached to the ground with various clothes-pegs and washing-lines. I was told that in the last evictions it had taken the bailiffs five hours to dismantle one particular plastic dwelling.

But even if the benders were stronger than they appeared to be, could some suicidal young American woman really benefit from coming to live in them?

Having secretly laughed at the notion, I later wondered if the women might not be right. It would be difficult to indulge in depression on the camps. They were much too depressing – much too near to the reality of the warheads. They didn't encourage states of mind which were unaffected by external circumstances.

The women were very good to any members of their camps who were ill. They'd been very patient and helpful to the hysteric at Green Gate. On one of the camps I'd seen a mongol girl and I couldn't imagine what she was doing there. I wondered if she'd soon be spotted by a hostile photographer and presented as a typical Greenham woman.

Eventually I found out that the mongol had been brought to the missile base by a psychiatric nurse who had looked after her since she was a baby. When this nurse had made her decision to make a protest on Greenham Common, she'd felt morally bound to bring this girl with her because she was the only person who could understand her signals. The mongol pottered around, seemingly very happy, on the camp. She collected wood all day long and she'd learnt how to keep the fire going. She had found a role that made her valuable, and the community was grateful for her efforts and she looked as if their approbation made her proud. When the soldiers called her a 'silly cunt', she went on collecting wood, quite immune to their derision. She was strong in the face of abuse. No amount of taunting could make this girl angry. She couldn't understand a word of it.

If the hysteric and the mongol had benefited from the tolerance and support of the Greenham women, maybe the American's daughter really could be made to feel less suicidal if she was to fly over from the United States and move in with her mother at Main Gate. It seemed possible that all the adrenalin that was released by the harsh battle for physical survival on the camps might give her some kind of strength with which she could fight off her black and self-destructive moods.

3

The threat of eviction was making the women of Main Gate edgy the first day that I went there. They looked at every passing truck with apprehension, fearing it might be the bailiffs. They hid some of their most precious possessions in the woods so that they wouldn't be pulped in the 'scruncher'.

'But can they just take your personal possessions and destroy them? Is that legal?' I asked.

They doubted that it was legal, but they assumed their belongings would be pulped anyway. As usual, they were fatalistic.

'I've had everything I own taken away from me before,' a student of Japanese studies told me. 'But even if they take everything away again, I'll never leave. I'll just sit here with nothing.'

I wondered if it was the women's ability to survive the loss of all material comforts that was one of the reasons that they were feared and hated.

'If you have nothing to lose, you can't really lose,' another woman said to me. It was this attitude that gave them their strength.

It was the fear that always accompanied the anger they aroused that mystified me. What was so frightening about a small group of pacifist women? When they were driven out of their camps and their shelters and their possessions were stripped away from them, they seemed like victims. Were they feared and disliked because their role aroused feelings that every individual recognized as unacceptable, the nasty desire to victimize the victim further?

Even if they were threatened by imprisonment and the

loss of their freedom, the threat held less than normal terror for women who had already lost their lives and freedom, in the sense that they had sacrificed their families and their professions and most of the things they cared about.

Even the threat of the real loss of their lives had less than usual terror for these women, who were convinced that their lives were about to be taken from them anyway. The death they saw themselves as condemned to if they had the ill-luck to be a nuclear survivor was such a long, drawn-out and agonizing one that it amounted to death after prolonged torture.

When Newbury council tried to scare them away from the missile base by threatening to seize their plastic cups and their tea-bags, it was a very small-minded approach to human beings who felt they were already facing the unendurable, for they foresaw the inevitable destruction of their children.

It was the acceptance that they were helpless to change the destructive course of all the governments who ignored the misery and unemployment of their people as they sunk the financial resources of the nation into death-dealing weapons that had made these women angry. It was a helpless anger that had given them the courage to put up a symbolic fight. If nothing was to be gained by their struggle, they knew certainly that nothing could be lost. By their symbolic presence on Greenham Common, they hoped to act as the voice of the millions of people all over the world who recognized that they had no voice.

The women's protest outside the Cruise missile base was a protest of feeling rather than a political one. It had a common-sense approach which could not be palmed off with any sophisticated reassurances of the power of 'deterrents' and the importance of military mastery. It had assumptions and convictions so basic that they could easily be dismissed as simplistic. It was the protest of all the women who have ever looked after children. It gave a black warning that came direct from personal experience. 'If you let children play with dangerous instruments, it won't be very long before there is a hideous accident.'

No one has ever liked warnings. Cassandra was not a popular figure and eventually she died because no one would believe her. The mother is always seen as a tiresome old fusspot and spoilsport whenever she tells the small boys not to play on the roof. The Greenham women were quite prepared to take on all the hostility and derision that their role was traditionally bound to arouse. Scorn and hostility could neither ruffle nor deter them, just as it never deterred the suffragettes when English society considered them pathetic, unfeminine figures of fun as they chained themselves to the railings.

The Greenham women had given up caring that they had the most disgusting public image. Many of their supporters wished they could be made to care more. They wished the young girls wouldn't paint their faces with webs and wear punk hair-styles. They wished the lesbians could be persuaded to be more restrained. But the peace women felt all these considerations were really immaterial and frivolous. What did it matter how they dressed? What did it matter what any of them were like as individuals? They had never claimed to be plaster saints. They were not trying to set fashions for *Vogue*. All that mattered was their position, which they believed to be a sane and pure one.

They were violently opposed to the way that the major world economies were so brutally geared to killing. They were not anti-American, as was often imagined because they were demonstrating in front of a missile that came from the United States. They loathed all the warlike policies of the Soviet Union. They had tried to send a delegation to the Kremlin. Just when the whole trip was planned, their visas were cancelled. They believed that the Soviet military officials had a horror of suddenly finding their country swarming with Greenham-type Russian women.

Realizing it was hopeless to try and make their protest behind the Iron Curtain, they had set up their camps in a country that still had a democracy. They hoped that a few intelligent people would get their simple message. They found it barbarous that humanity was devoting its wealth and talent to destructive ends rather than improving life on the planet.

The Greenham women also refused to care about their public image because the whole concept of the concocted, deodorized image was obnoxious to them. They felt that it was only suitable for TV stars and politicians. They despised all conformist images, seeing them as one more horrible product of the common passion for evading reality. They believed it was the refusal to face up to the terrifying reality that was placing all our lives in such danger.

They had a favourite analogy of the endangered Arctic explorer. He has to fight the overwhelming desire to lie down in the snow and shut his eyes. If he once lets himself shut his eyes, he will die.

The Greenham women felt that too many people were shutting their eyes in the snow – that they found it much easier not to think about the inevitable end-product of all the frenetic international manufacturing of weapons.

As they tried to wake the sleepers in the snow, the peace women recognized that their role was bound to be very unpopular. The sleeper hates to be woken. He hates to be alerted to his peril. His terror, and his fury at the terror that he feels, can project itself. The figure who points out the danger can seem like the danger itself.

The peace women were certain that even if they had presented the most dainty public image (which would have been extremely difficult, what with all the mud and the lack of facilities of the camps), even if they had achieved this respectable housewife projection and expelled every lesbian and every girl with red punk hair from their camps, they would have aroused just as much general loathing.

While they sat in front of the Cruise missile drawing attention to the danger in which humanity had placed itself, they were bound to draw all the fire of the public's buried terror and anger at the nuclear monster. In the past, the innocent messenger who brought bad tidings was seen as the enemy and he was killed. The tidings the peace women brought were very bad indeed.

*

In the camps I was often reminded of the last war. Particularly at night there was the same feeling of being in the blitz. Everyone made tea and tried to remain over-cheerful, in order to keep up morale. Many of the women sat up most of the night because it was useless for them to try to sleep. When the helicopters came zooming down to 'buzz' them, they made an earsplitting roar, and it gave one the sense of being in serious danger from the air.

As the camps were so close to the 'bomb', whenever there was a loud noise in the night it gave one a shock that was more unconscious than rational. 'Oh, my God! The missile is exploding!'

As well as having a wartime mood, the peace camps also had a curious hospital atmosphere. They were like a Mad Hatter's hospital in which everything had gone awry and yet some of the formal routines were still retained. The hospital feeling seemed strange until one remembered that many of the Greenham women had medical training. At Main Gate, at night, the campers begged one to be quiet. 'Please don't wake the baby.' 'Please remember that some of the women may be sleeping.'

There were signs all round the camps. 'Please leave things as you would like to find them.'

I heard an elderly lady asking the women if her husband would be allowed to sit round the fire at 'Indigo'. Apparently he was a peace movement supporter.

'He can sit here with us in the daytime. But I'm afraid he'll have to leave once it starts to get dark.' It was the reply of matron announcing the rules that protected her patients.

The bender that I was lent by the women was known as the Ritz and also as 'Hag's Hotel'. It really was a Ritz of a bender. It was tucked away deep in a gorse thicket. The prickles of the gorse had been removed and the stems provided the foundations on which the dwelling had been constructed by a cunning drape of polythene and rugs which were held down by washing lines.

Hag's Hotel had a wooden floor raised from the ground which already made it seem a Ritz compared to the low rabbit-burrow benders which got all the ground frost and made the women feel they had to choose between suffocating or freezing, because polythene lets in no air. But even with its raised flooring, the blanket that acted as the carpet of Hag's Hotel was soaking wet from rising damp.

The Ritz was lent to guests and it was a storing place for the peace women's blankets and candles and clothes. Once again, it had the business-like hospital-type notices. 'If you store your things here, please label them.' 'The contents are communal. Take what you need.' 'If this bender is used irresponsibly, it will close to the public.'

It felt very unreal crouching with a candle in the Ritz, deep in the gorse bushes. On one level, it was like hiding away in a children's secret tree-house, except it wasn't any fun being there. Comparatively comfortable as it was, I soon started to suffer from panic and claustrophobia. Every time there was a creak, I thought it was a vandal from Newbury arriving with a load of maggots or a red-hot poker. The gorse that surrounded the bender seemed dangerous. It would be so easy for anyone who hated the women to set it on fire.

A Scottish woman came into the bender and sat with me. She was an expert on soil analysis and she had two young children whom she'd left with her husband. She told me that her family had found it very hard at first when she'd left them to live at Greenham. Her husband had thought he couldn't manage, but finally he was starting to get used to it.

She gave the sad, resigned shrug that meant she felt she had no alternative but to leave her children and live on the base. If they suffered from her absence, she felt that was better than having dead or mutilated children.

Her conviction that by sitting in the dark in a gorse thicket, she could save her children was mysterious to me and I could only marvel at her optimism.

She believed that the message from Greenham was very slowly spreading and that people who had never worried that they might be given leukaemia by some accidental leak of radioactivity were starting to think about it. She thought

39

they were also starting to realize there would be no winners in a nuclear war. The tiny Scottish village that she came from had sent £100 to the women on Greenham Common.

'That's a *huge* sum for them,' she said. 'They never think about politics and nukes up there. The whole village is three stone cottages and a post office. It all seems far, too far, away from them.'

We both went back to join the other women round the fire. We were getting frozen in the Ritz. It seemed far preferable to sit up rather than to lie down on the hard, damp surface of its floor.

How do these women bear the nights? I wondered. How do they manage to get through the days knowing that they can only end in more agonizing nights of fear and sleeplessness? The stoicism of the peace campers astonished me. They regarded it as a job that had to be done – and they just got on with it.

It was bad dreams that had driven many of them to make their protest at the site of the missile – recurring dreams that were so nightmarish that it made them realize their unconscious was giving expression to a terror they hardly dared to feel.

Once they started to face the terror under which they were living, they found it intolerable that they should be made to live in a state of constant pointless fear. They felt their lives were being ruined by the nuclear threat which prevented them from seeing any real point in devoting their energies to raising children, or pursuing activities that could be beneficial to their society.

Before they came to Greenham Common, they had sometimes tried to express the feeling of paralysis that the threat of nuclear extinction gave them. They were told they were being hysterical, that they were silly, ignorant women who were too stupid to understand the protection they were being given by the complex Western defence system. They still found it impossible to have faith in the untested theory that deterrents give humanity endless safety. They failed to understand why so many people were blindly prepared to accept this theory as if it was a religious faith.

In the camps round the base, they found it a relief that their pessimistic terrors were shared rather than ridiculed. They were terrified by the knowledge that a 'limited nuclear war' in Europe would cause the death of one hundred million people, that in a full scale war between the USA and USSR, all life on earth could be destroyed and the planet would be plunged into darkness.

Their terrors had not been allayed by the statements of the world leaders. 'We're satisfied to be able to finish off the United States first time round. Once is quite enough. What good does it do to annihilate a country twice? We're not a bloodthirsty people.'

Nikita Khrushchev's announcement had terrified the women and they had not been reassured by the statements of the Russian leaders who had succeeded him.

They were also alarmed by Ronald Reagan's announcement that he believes that Armageddon will come in this generation. They were frightened by the fundamentalist attitude which he shares with the powerful American evangelical leader Jerry Falwell, who is his strong supporter. Falwell has prophesied that 'in less than sixty years there will be some nuclear holocaust, a war in which Russia will be destroyed with nuclear weapons, but Christians living in Russia will be "raptured", that is transported physically to heaven in a twinkling of an eye, and will be saved from the holocaust in this way.'

When Ronald Reagan announced that 'the point of reading the Bible is to realize that this world and our lives don't really belong to us. What the Good Lord wants from each of us and from this world is up to Him, not you and me', the Greenham women felt his position was dangerously close to the position of Jerry Falwell. They were also frightened of Caspar Weinberger, the American Secretary of Defense, when he said 'I have read the Book of Revelations and yes, I believe the world is going to end – by an act of God I hope – but every day I think that time is running out.'

On Greenham Common, the women shared a terror of the attitude that regards the holocaust as inevitable. They thought it immoral to try and forget the terrible descriptions and photographs of Hiroshima and Nagasaki.

They had come to the base at Greenham in order to remind the world that the Cruise missile can carry a warhead ten times stronger than the bombs that devastated these cities, that 160 of these missiles will be sited in Great Britain, that the British people has not voted for their presence.

They were not only protesting that Britain had put herself in a position in which a 'limited nuclear war' could be fought out on her soil without the consultation of her government, they had come to Greenham to represent the terror that they believed was widely felt, and often not expressed because those who voiced it were made to feel unpatriotic or insane.

By symbolically representing this terror, they hoped to give courage to all those who were taking the position of ostriches out of fear of ridicule.

As I watched them sitting round their bad fires with only candles for lighting, I was again reminded of a hospital. Nurses have always sat up all night and made tea while they keep vigil beside the bed of the dying patient. Now it was the planet that these women saw as dying and they sat up all night with the selflessness of the nurse. Many of them were real nurses and they behaved as if they were on duty.

'Whoops a daisy!' a jolly middle-aged woman said as the kettle fell off the log on which it was precariously perching.

There were moments when it could all seem normal in the camps, even at night. The women filled hot-water bottles and clung to them to keep themselves warm. The conversation would become very ordinary as the women chatted about this and that. They found jeans hopeless for wear on the camps. The fibre retained water. Orange peel made surprisingly good kindling if you dried it out, for the oils that it contained made it burn very easily. When they exchanged these housewifely hints, it could all seem cosy and normal.

Yet the camps were far from cosy and it was most abnormal that these women should be sitting around in these atrocious conditions that guaranteed insomnia – not from any necessity – but from choice.

4

On Greenham Common one was constantly provided with a series of disturbing images. They rippled through one's mind like the unreal sequences of nightmare.

I was standing outside Main Gate, when some American children came out of the base in a coach that was taking them to school. The children saw me standing there and seeing any woman as their enemy, they all put out their tongues and made 'fuck you' signs with their fingers. This ugly little display of hatred from such small children was horrible. The hatred that seethed round the Cruise missile was always expressed in sexual terms and the American children had clearly learnt their lesson.

'I just loathe seeing children going in and out of that base,' a peace woman said to me. 'It seems so wrong to bring them up in there. I find that really evil.'

Another startling image was provided by the hunt. The entrance to the base had a lane leading down to a busy and dangerous main road lying at right angles to it.

Along this fast and crowded main road a hunt suddenly appeared in full cry. It was such an unlikely place for anyone to choose to hunt that for a second I thought I was having a hallucination.

In contrast to the greyness and the khaki colours of the base, the hunt provided an amazing splash of colour. It was like seeing a scene from an old-fashioned sporting print surrealistically superimposed on to a military setting of juggernauts and jeeps.

The master looked resplendent in his black silk top hat, his scarlet coat and spotless white breeches, and gleaming top boots. He was followed by his whippers-in who were also dressed in scarlet. After the riders in red coats there came all the other members of the hunt with their bowler hats; all the resolute horsey ladies in formal hunting gear with their hair neatly tucked into hair-nets.

Everything about this privileged cavalcade looked impeccable until one realized that there was something very peculiar about this hunt. The horses were going all over the road. No one was making any attempt to keep them on to the verge.

The hunt brought all the military traffic that was hoping to enter the base to an angry semi-standstill. The drivers started shouting and hooting their horns. The hounds were weaving through the motor bikes and missing them by inches.

The highly-strung thoroughbreds were terrified of all the hooting and the screeching brakes and were stumbling and slipping about on the wet tarmac with their legs in very great danger. If one of them was to take a fall on that unsuitable surface, it would most likely have to be shot.

What could have happened to this hunt which seemed to have forgotten all its most precious rules? The lives of the hounds were at risk in the dense military traffic, and the horses looked so frantic that there seemed a very great danger that one of them might shy and throw its rider under a truck.

It was only when I saw the reaction of the Greenham women that the behaviour of this foolhardy hunt was explained.

I had not realized how violently anti blood sports the women were. They left their fire and ran down to the side of the road. They started shouting 'shame!' and they shook their fists at the scarlet-coated master. It was the first time I'd seen any of them show hysteria.

Watching this unlikely scene, I was terrified that the cries of the women would further petrify the horses and make them bolt, causing some terrible accident for which they would be blamed as murderesses.

It shocked me that the master appeared not to care at all if this happened. It was as if he felt that any misadventure that befell either his followers or his hounds would be in a good cause. He was determined to upset the Greenham women and he appeared to be prepared to take any risk to do so.

He started cracking his whip in a crazy unhuntsman-like fashion. There was something very cruel and deranged in his whipping. He was showing the women what he would like to do to them.

He wouldn't move his hunt from the strip of military main road in front of their camps. He seemed to feel obliged to remain in their view, defiantly parading the scarlet of a coat which they saw as bloodstained.

The Americans, in their great trucks, soon started to get very fed up with this annoying hunt. They also knew how to upset the Greenham women. They could buzz them with helicopters and use other modern methods. If the peace women were to be harassed, they wanted it done their way.

The US military were not impressed by John Peel, however gay his coat might be, when he blocked the entrance to their missile. The hunt was made to move on by the military police.

'That wasn't a real hunt,' one of the peace women said to me. 'That was a provocation.'

Just as she spoke, something very startling happened. The master reappeared, galloping recklessly along the slippery tarmac of the main road. He apparently felt that he hadn't sufficiently outraged the Greenham women and he'd come back to make a final demonstration of his superiority and power. He turned into the lane that lay between the women's benders. We had to jump out of the way of his horse which he was riding as if he was engaged in a military charge. When you are on foot, any horse that charges you seems enormous and ferocious, and almost more deadly than a tank.

It was doubtful that this huntsman could have stopped his horse if he'd wanted to. It was also doubtful that he would have wanted to stop, seeing two hated women standing stupidly in his path.

As I watched the master completing his cavalry charge through the benders, I felt I was watching a man who'd taken temporary leave of his senses. He couldn't really think there was a fox lurking in all the traffic congestion of Main Gate. He didn't appear to be thinking at all. That was why he was dangerous. He was seeing red. Rage against the Greenham women had sent so much blood to his head that he'd lost all sense of responsibility.

When he got up to the actual gate of the base, he was forced to turn. The paratroopers were not going to allow him to enter. They didn't want him to continue his furious tally-ho charge round and round the warheads. A fox with true cunning could have taken advantage of this situation and formed his own little peace lair within the military confines of Cruise missile.

The peace women booed the huntsman as he turned. They continued to boo him until he became a tiny spot of angry red as he vanished, galloping along the grey wire of the perimeter.

'Nukes and bloodsports – it's all the same mentality,' one of the Greenham women said. She suddenly then gave a little scream. 'Oh, my God, look what that silly idiot has done!'

It was certainly idiotic what the master had done. In the excitement of his charge through the benders, he'd completely forgotten one of his prime responsibilities. He'd abandoned his hounds and they were baying and yelping with terror as they went weaving blindly through the now fast-moving traffic of the mainroad.

The women couldn't bear watching the plight of the hounds as they risked more and more nerve-wracking near-misses with the wheels of aircraft carriers and motor bikes. They went into the road and formed a cordon to halt the traffic. It was ironic that the lives of the hounds were being protected by the Greenham women and not by the master. It was ominous that round the missile base, feelings of hate ran so high that all basic rules of behaviour were forgotten. Hunts ceased to conduct themselves as normal hunts. British sportsmen ceased to be sporting. The legs of their thoroughbreds, the welfare of their hounds, all seemed to be forgotten in the war against the Greenham women.

The sleepy, peaceful, provincial town of Newbury always seemed strange after leaving the camps. In the main hotel, tweeded men with puce complexions talked endlessly about racing and they sat in the lobby and they read *Horse and Hound*, and *Farmers Weekly*. They looked so robust, and confident and in control as they concentrated on their rural pursuits. They didn't seem to give a thought about the base – or its implications.

I bought all the local newspapers in order to try and understand the mood of the town. I read the complaint of an irate reader who implored the editor that he never again be made to read one more boring word about the Greenham women. Was there nothing more interesting in the world that the papers could report? His question had a desperation. The Newbury residents were clearly not as indifferent to the issue of the Cruise missile as they superficially appeared.

If this irate figure didn't want to read about the peace women, he was certainly out of luck. The Greenham women had become a local obsession. There were innumerable items about them on every single newspaper page. There were features on their imminent evictions, reports on their arrests on charges of breaches of the peace. There were endless descriptions of their trials, their fines, and their prison sentences. The Newbury *Weekly News* had received so many letters about the peace women they were running an extra letter page.

The hysteria of the Newbury letter columns at the time of the evictions was totally disproportionate to the real effect the women were having on the community. A visitor to the town would never have known these little camps tucked away on the Common existed. There was a recurring accusation and complaint that the peace women had created 'eyesores'. But the unaesthetic appearance of their camps only affected the unlucky people whose houses directly faced the perimeter fence. Since the arrival of the base, these particular houses looked on to all the vast tangles of barbed wire that covered the desecrated Common. They could be said to be already facing an eyesore. Their owners were complaining about the hair on the wart.

In the period after the announcement of the eviction orders on the peace women, to judge by the local newspapers the issue of the camps on Greenham Common had split the town in two. A woman wrote in to say that she had never been more ashamed of coming from Newbury than when she saw the way that the town was persecuting the peace women.

'What a pity that Newbury will be seen in such a bad light in our children's and grandchildren's history books, that is, if this beautiful earth of ours is to have a history beyond the 1980s,' she wrote. She ended her letter with the resolute sentence, 'I can no longer call myself a Newburian.'

Another local resident compared the efforts of the Greenham women to those of Jesus Christ. 'It's almost two thousand years since someone tried to promote the cause of peace and love. He left home and family and obviously suffered rejection, for he said: "The birds of the air have nests, foxes have holes, but the Son of Man has nowhere to lay his head." Well, we all know what happened to him. But somehow his message gained strength ... Women today who leave home and family and turn the other cheek and offer no aggression are reviled, evicted and persecuted. Their enemies invite support from those who wish the means for world destruction to be in their belligerent hands.'

Monseigneur Bruce Kent also wrote to the Newbury *Weekly News* to support the women. He praised their courage for continuing, in very harsh conditions and sometimes in the face of mindless hatred, to bear witness, and remind the country that nuclear weapons are both illegal and immoral.

He felt that far from increasing our security, Cruise missiles make the present situation more and more unstable. 'Had there been such a witness as the Greenham women outside the concentration camps of Hitler's Germany in the early thirties perhaps millions of Jews, pacifists, political "undesirables", homosexuals, and gypsies would not have gone to their dreadful death. No doubt "respectable" Germans at the time would have complained in just the way that some, but by no means all, the residents of Newbury are doing today. Thank God for the many others who offer the hand of friendship, concern, and love.'

These favourable attitudes towards the peace women were certainly not the only ones represented in the Newbury newspapers. A group of residents had recently formed a group which called itself RAGE, and it was appealing for supporters. These inflamatory initials stood for Ratepayers Against Greenham Encampments.

This newly formed society had just taken out a huge advertisement in the Newbury *Weekly News*. 'It is time that the residents of Newbury and district joined together in organized efforts to rid themselves of these squatters,' read the announcement. The advertisement had the most awful picture of a fat and hideous woman with boils and protruding balloon breasts sitting astride a phallic missile and holding a piece of barbed wire in one hand and an olive branch in the other.

'Send a Greenham Camper on a Cruise this summer,' read the caption.

The unappealing Greenham woman, as depicted in the RAGE cartoon, was wearing a crucifix as an ear-ring. Was this meant to indicate that a Christian symbol on a peace woman was a blasphemy? Or was it laughing at the women because some of them were Christians?

The whole advertisement had a very violent and sexually smutty tone. But it was clear from the local papers that RAGE had many supporters.

'Sheer weight of local public opinion is vital and necessary to bring more and more pressure on the district councils to have these atrocious law-breaking trespassers removed. They have for far too long caused endless hardship to residents in and around the Greenham area ... I hope that the silent majority will support RAGE,' wrote in a woman who signed herself by the fierce name of Betty Warr.

The chairman of RAGE, Anthony Meyer, found Monseigneur Bruce Kent's letter praising the women 'shameful'. He reminded him that Greenham women 'wallow in filth, create massive waste of public money, abuse our police and legal system ... If cleanliness is next to Godliness, Mr Kent should look at the state of the "ladies" at Newbury police courts to realize how far from God his flock has strayed.'

In another letter to the Newbury *Weekly News*, the RAGE chairman denied that pigs' blood had been thrown at the women in the peace camps. He said that the only blood on the camps was their own.

There were readers who complained about the obscenity of the RAGE cartoon. It reminded them of the way the Nazis used to portray the Jews.

The spokesman for RAGE, Mr Learoyd, defended the caricature and said his organization had deliberately made the drawing of the Greenham woman light and humorous in tone. Later, when he showed it to me personally, I examined it very carefully and I failed to see that it was either light or humorous. I thought it a drawing that had been sketched by a pen dipped in poison and hatred. But that was only the way that I saw it, and it was the differing ways in which the people of Newbury saw the peace women that was creating such an impassioned correspondence in the local newspapers. It was this clash of view that was making life so wretched for the unfortunate irate reader who only longed not to have to read about the Greenham women.

In the bar of the main hotel in Newbury I met a jovial man. He was middle-aged and his cheeks were streaked scarlet from over-drinking. He looked as if he was a typical 'Newburian' ratepayer and I got into conversation, hoping to find out how he felt about the missile base and the defeat of the Greenham women.

He was an antique dealer and he turned out to be a *bon viveur* and quite a wiseacre. He told me about every pub and bar in Newbury. Some had 'good' atmospheres, some had 'bad'. Some of the bad ones were good in the sense that they sold you a pint of beer that was cheaper.

Originally, this man came from the North of England, but he now considered himself a 'Newburian'.

'For me, there is nowhere that can touch Newbury,' he said. 'Give me Newbury every time. There is not a place in England where you can find the lovely weather you get around here.'

The rain was smashing down against the window of the hotel bar, but he seemed blithely unaware of it. I had just come from the cold of the camps and I'd had little evidence of the lovely local climate that he was boasting about. I wondered whether from the special perspective of the warm interiors of all the Newbury pubs and bars that he inhabited, he got the happy impression that he was living in tropical conditions.

I asked him what he thought of the Greenham peace women. He didn't know much about them. Most of the pubs and bars that he frequented wouldn't let them in. The women he had met hadn't seemed 'bad' women.

'But if only they would dress better and wash more. A woman who doesn't dress nicely dishonours herself, don't you think?'

I explained that it was very difficult to wash in the camps, that the women only had bottled water. He seemed rather shocked to hear this. He hadn't realized they had no water.

'Oh, that's not fair on them not to have water. The council really ought to let them have water.'

I asked him why he thought they were so hated by some of the Newbury ratepayers. This genial beer-drinking rate-payer didn't seem to have been at all affected by the presence of the women at the base. He showed no sign of having suffered any of the 'hardship' that Betty Warr had described in her letter.

He said the women had brought down the value of the houses around Greenham Common – this made people very angry with them.

'We have lovely homes in Newbury. We have some of the loveliest homes in England. Oh, yes, we really have lovely homes in Newbury.' He was a man who liked to repeat all his sentences as if he hoped by repetition to introduce profundity.

He told me that some of the residents of Newbury also resented the peace women because they were preventing the Americans from shopping in the town. This seemed oversensitive of the Americans. Many of the shops in Newbury refused to allow the peace women to enter their premises because they claimed they smelt. They insisted they had to protect their customers. There was very little risk of the Americans bumping into them with their food trolleys.

Surely the US military attached to the missile couldn't be so fastidious that they were unable to bear to pass the benders in their Cadillacs? They could drive past the women's camps in one flash. They needn't get more than a brief whiff of the women. It all seemed very mysterious.

Eventually I discovered the whole thing was total nonsense. The Americans had a large supermarket within the base which was much more convenient for them and much cheaper than shopping in Newbury. It was convenience and economy rather than the Greenham women which prevented them from shopping in the local town. Even in the most trivial matters, the peace protestors were made scapegoats.

The antique dealer then told me that some of the local residents objected to the Greenham women because they were always cutting holes in the perimeter fence. He then lowered his voice and he leant towards me as though confiding an astonishing secret. 'I'll tell you something,' he whispered. 'There are very prominent people in Newbury who secretly support what the women are doing. Oh, yes, there are very prominent people in this town who don't really care what the women do to the bloody perimeter fence. They really don't give a damn what happens to it. You see, there are very prominent people with beautiful houses in this town and they *hate* the base, they hate the base much more than they hate the women. They don't want anything to happen to their houses. Most of us here in Newbury hate the American base, if the truth was really told. You couldn't really like the base – now could you?'

I asked him if he thought the new eviction orders would be the end of the women's peace protest.

'Oh, good Lord, no!' he said. 'You can evict those women as much as you like – but you'll never see the end of them.'

He was making them sound mythical – invincible.

'Maybe the people who want to evict those women are really jealous of them!' he conjectured.

Having made this statement, the antique dealer said he was going up the road to some pub where the atmosphere was much more lively. He asked me to join him, but I preferred to remain in the hotel bar. I wanted to think about the prominent people of Newbury who were concerned that their houses might be damaged in a possible nuclear holocaust.

Just before he left he suddenly wagged his finger at me with the same wiseacre roguishness with which he'd told me where I could find cheaper pints of beer in the Newbury pubs.

'They really may be jealous!' He gave a mischievous wink. 'I think that may be it! I think that here in Newbury, we none of us like those women because in our hearts we are all bloody jealous of them. In our hearts we know we haven't got the guts to do what the women are doing.'

The antique dealer went off in the rain, which he presumably wouldn't notice. It was nice to think he would find good Newbury weather in some pub with a lively atmosphere.

6

The next time I went back to Blue Gate, there was no sign of Pat, but a lot of young girls with shaven heads and central tufts of multi-coloured 'Mohican' hair were sitting round the fire of her desolate 'living-room'.

To the conventional old-world eyes of Newbury, radical hair-dos made their owners seem dangerous. Old guard 'Newburians' could not accept that the way that these girls wore their hair was only the current style of the very young, that it no more indicated bad character than the 'bob' that scandalized older people in the 1920s.

In London, the 'Mohican' look was accepted, but once it was moved to the provinces, and particularly to the controversial peace camps, it gave fuel to the idea that the camps were inhabited by fierce and foreign tribeswomen.

The new little group at Blue Gate were very polite and friendly. Considering how nerve-wracked, exhausted and harassed the women always felt, their good manners were astonishing. The sleepless, hungry, shivering girls would get up to offer their most comfortable seat of damp cardboard to any visiting older woman. Although the state of their food supplies was often abysmal, they always offered the best they had to the newcomer. They had created a very altruistic little community on the camps. When visitors dropped off their gifts of food and money at one of the gates on the base, they always looked lost and confounded when they realized there was no particular woman who was meant to receive it. 'Oh, give it to anyone,' they'd be told. 'Thank you very much. It's really kind of you.'

New visitors often looked seriously alarmed by what

seemed to them like off-handedness and irresponsibility. But all the provisions that the Greenham women received were scrupulously shared out. Within their limited and pooled resources, the needs of every single woman on the camps were invariably met.

Some of the gates tended to receive more donations because geographically they were more accessible to the cars that kept arriving from all over England. But the women had set up a system by which they went tramping the exhausting round of the perimeter, always checking to see that the more far-flung camps were not lacking in salt, firewood, candles, sugar – all such basic necessities.

In the morning they had established a routine for distributing the letters the women received. Two of the young women would set off from Main Gate, which was the only camp where mail could be received. They'd do the exhausting and dreary tour of the perimeter, dropping off the letters at all the camps. Sometimes, after their morning walk, they would discover they had not delivered a longed-for letter from some woman's child or husband or lover. They had wasted their energies carrying hate-mail. These letters were always very nasty little missives. They were almost invariably obscene. They often came from the home towns of the peace campers, from neighbours who hated their pacifist position and disapproved of their presence on the Common.

'Is Pat around?' I asked the girls at Blue Gate.

'Do you mean older Pat?'

I imagined that I did, but they probably had many Pats on the base.

Apparently older Pat wasn't well. She was knitting in her sleeping bender. I couldn't see how she could knit in any of the low polythene constructions on her camp. Blue Gate had particularly low and unappetizing benders. Some of the other camps had built taller ones so it was possible to crouch in them upright, but the benders at Blue Gate were built so close to the ground that I could only imagine the unfortunate Pat as lying like a kitten, doing cat's-cradle on her back.

I sat down at the fire and I was told that they'd all had a terrible night with the soldiers.

What sort of night had the peace women had? That was always the most important question on the camps. A bad night is an ominous sign for the very ill and suggests less hope for their survival. The nights of the women were nearly always atrocious.

'They just wouldn't stop,' one of the young women told me. She made a gesture over her shoulders, indicating the soldiers who, as usual, were glaring at the camps from behind the perimeter. The women deliberately tried not to look at the military. They usually sat with their backs to them. Sometimes it seemed as if the soldiers treated them with such infantile hostility because they felt rejected by these women who spurned the great phallic symbol of the missile. But that was surely too simplistic.

The military had been given orders not to have any 'eye contact' with the women. This resembled the ancient instructions that used to be given to Catholic nuns when they were exhorted to keep 'custody of the eyes'. This military order treated the paratroopers as if they were maidenly creatures who could be led astray by a lascivious glance. This was unexpected, yet it was no more unlikely than the curious situation on the perimeter where British men and women spent night after night so very close to each other and yet remained on such different ideological sides of the fence that although both sexes saw themselves as defending their country, they feared and despised each other as destroyers and traitors.

'Aren't you ashamed?' the women would ask the British police as they watched them ushering American military personnel into the base. The police would look angry and wounded, as many men look when subjected to female criticism. They looked as if it was the lack of female approval they would have liked to have put under arrest, rather than the actual women.

'You ought to be ashamed of yourselves,' the British police would growl as they watched supporters carrying chocolates and jam and Brillo pads to the women.

The supporters were not ashamed of the cakes and candles that they had brought to the camps. Their shame was different. They felt ashamed of their lack of courage and their inability to make any personal sacrifice to a cause they believed in.

I watched an old, white-haired lady from Bristol arrive at the camps. It was the first time she had been to Greenham and when she saw the hideous conditions that the women were living in, she burst into tears. 'I feel you are doing this for all of us,' she said. She had brought them some bread which she had baked herself and she had enriched it with molasses because she thought that it would be good for the health of the women.

There was a great health consciousness in the gifts that were brought by the supporters. The women always received a lot of oranges because the donors liked the idea that they were getting vitamin C. They were brought apples because they were good for cleaning the teeth, as lack of water was such a problem in the camps and apples were meant to keep the doctor away. They were brought soups which had been prepared with enormous thought as to their nutritional value. The admirers of the women tended to treat them as if they were growing children who needed calcium for their bones, and iron for their blood.

Yet the women who supported them knew that even if they poured all their hearts and energies into enriching the bread that they brought to the camps, molasses was not really enough. The Greenham women needed the support of their presence on the camps, not their bread, however enriched it might be. Yet it never seemed to be the intention of the Greenham women to make their visitors feel guilty as they dropped off their gifts at the derelict camps as if they were bringing offerings to the temple.

The women's attitude was a tolerant one and they were simply grateful to their sympathisers for doing as much as they could do. They accepted that many women supported their position and yet were psychologically incapable of bringing them more than tokens. They didn't blame them for this, they accepted it as a fact.

It was not the Greenham women, it was the situation, that made their supporters feel such guilt as they sailed off in their cars and went back to their comforts, leaving the women to face another appalling night.

They felt guilty for allowing the Greenham women to be like the sappers who are pushed forward ahead of the army. The Greenham women were taking all the risks. They had gone into the dangerous territory where all the mines were buried and their supporters only followed them like straggling military units with very bad discipline and even worse morale.

While I was sitting at Blue Gate hoping that Pat would feel better and come out of her bender, one of the girls told me she'd done something awful in the night – that she'd done a custard attack.

I had no idea what she meant. A custard attack could have been punk slang for any kind of criminal act. She seemed rather upset about it. I asked her what she'd done.

'You know we only got out of the nick yesterday,' she said. 'Holloway is really hell. It's a different hell from the camps, but it's hell all the same.'

'Why were you in Holloway?' I asked.

She gave the resigned Greenham shrug. 'Breach of the peace. Damage to the bloody perimeter.'

She said that last night when the 'squaddies', as the women called the RAF squadrons that defended the missile, had become impossible, her nerves had been so raw after Holloway that she'd thought she'd go mad if these men wouldn't let her sleep. Something had snapped and she'd got some custard powder and brewed it up in the camp kettle. Once it cooled she had left the fire and crept out into the darkness. She'd thrown her brew of cold custard through the wire of the perimeter so that one of the 'squaddies' had his face and uniform drenched in custard. He had looked like a slapstick victim in a child's comic.

'What did he do?' I asked.

'He didn't do anything. He couldn't shoot me. He's not allowed to.'

She seemed ashamed that she had attacked someone who

was powerless to retaliate, for she kept giving reasons why she had done her attack as if she was trying to excuse it to herself rather than me.

'I think it was just getting out of Holloway. I think it was finding Pat was ill. I think it was knowing we are going to be evicted any moment now and not knowing where we can go.'

She appeared to be embarrassed that in the night she had broken the most important rule of the peace campers. 'Turn the other cheek to all manifestations of human violence.'

Sitting round the fire, there was another young woman who had painted her shaven head with exactly the same patterns of green and brown camouflage as the uniform worn by the paratroopers within the base. Her head reflected the base like the mirrors the women held up to it. Shaven heads were a practical style for the camps, although they helped to fan the hostility of the local residents, because they saw them as unfeminine. The Greenham women who wore their hair long found it difficult to dry after they'd shampooed it. Their fires were inadequate and as a result they caught many chills.

The young woman with the paratrooper's uniform head was called Liz. She said that the situation of the prisoners in Holloway had made her feel unbearably guilty. The whole experience had made her feel like a spoilt brat.

It was ironic that the Greenham women who made so many women feel guilty suffered in their turn from guilt.

'The whole prison is so sad,' she said. 'Most of the women there are black and unemployed and they are serving long sentences for pathetic little crimes such as prostitution and petty thieving. They were lovely to us. It was awful. They kept buying us presents – things like cigarettes – and their prison allowance is only £1.15 a week.'

She said that various prison reforms had come about when the middle-class suffragettes saw what the insides of the jails were like. She hoped the Greenham women would do something similar to improve the conditions.

'You feel those poor women will spend most of their lives

in Holloway,' she said. 'They've got nothing to go to when they get out.'

She hated to hear the Holloway prisoners screaming when they were put into solitary. 'They strip them naked just to humiliate them. If they make a fuss, they bring in men to strip them because they mind that more.'

She said she'd heard an old woman screaming her head off as she was being stripped and she'd asked one of the prison wardresses how she could bear her job. 'Do you know what she said? She found it fun. Can you imagine a woman having such a horrible attitude? That's what we are trying to fight here at Greenham. If that kind of horrible attitude rules the world, we have all had it.'

Another young woman said that she didn't think that being in Holloway was nearly as bad as being in hospital.

'I wouldn't have expected a nurse to say that,' Liz said to her.

The nurse insisted that Holloway wasn't nearly as bad as most hospitals – that you didn't feel quite so powerless. You didn't have needles stuck into you against your will. You weren't suddenly given enemas. In Holloway you didn't have a lot of students examining your wounds. You didn't have strangers hovering round and gaping at you when your legs were separated. You felt you were seen as more of a person and you weren't quite as badly humiliated in Holloway as you were in most of the hospitals where she'd worked.

Pat suddenly came out of her bender and joined us at the fire. She looked miserably unwell. She was coughing like a consumptive. She'd lost the invulnerable quality that she'd had before she fell ill. She now seemed an old woman who might easily die of exposure in these godforsaken camps.

'I don't know what the hell to do,' she said to me. 'My whole throat is infected and the infection's going down on my chest. It hurts me to breathe.'

She realized that her infection would never clear up in the cold of the camp. It seemed to be getting worse and worse. She realized that she needed an antibiotic – that the sensible thing would be to go home and stay with her son in the warm until the infection cleared up.

'I suppose it's really rather stupid to die in these camps,' she said. 'It's more important to stay alive in order to keep up the protest.'

Feeling so ill, she had worked herself into a state in which she almost seemed to feel that nuclear war might break out if she left the base.

She explained that the evictions were more serious at Blue Gate than they were at some of the other camps. At Main Gate, there were woods where the women could retreat to, but Blue Gate was surrounded by private property. She pointed at the red-brick stockbroker-style house with the two-car garage that was just across the road from the camp. 'The woman who owns that house hates us enough already,' Pat said. 'We can't really move our benders on to her lawn. That certainly wouldn't make her like us any more.'

She said that the situation of the women at Blue Gate was so serious that she was thinking of making an appeal for survival bags. I'd never heard of such bags, but they sounded a very desperate last resort for the women. She told me that there was a cheap kind of survival bag, but unfortunately they were not much good because they made you perspire so much that if you spent the night in one, you would wake up wringing wet. There was an expensive kind called Gortex which protected you from the rain and they had the advantage that they let in air. If the women went into Gortex bags, the bailiffs couldn't seize them and destroy them, for they were not meant to confiscate property which any individual had on their person.

Pat went into such a fit of violent coughing that it alarmed me. I longed for her to go back to her son's house. She was old and she was very ill and she obviously needed to be put in a warm bed and nursed. It was frightening to think of her going into a survival bag. But her needs didn't interest her. It was her wishes rather than her needs that had to be respected. Her wishes were to remain at the gate of the base so that the warheads could not go out into the countryside without anyone knowing it.

'If we don't get any Gortexes, I was wondering if we could move into the local church,' she said. 'Churches aren't meant to refuse to give sanctuary to the homeless.' She laughed as if she had little faith that the church would offer shelter to any Greenham women.

I couldn't imagine the respectable church-goers of Newbury being overjoyed to find their church full of peace women when they turned up for morning worship.

I asked her what she felt about the new organization RAGE. How would it affect the women on the camps?

'I don't know what they are planning to do to us – but it's bound to be bad. I'm sure that the whole idea of RAGE will make the vigilantes in Newbury feel they can make more attacks on us. They'll like the idea that the community approves of it. There is so much hate about. It's really horrible. Can you imagine anyone starting an organization called RAGE?'

She said she was feeling so ill she thought she would have to go and lie down. 'I find it a defeat, but I may have to be sensible and go home for a while.'

Pat went off to lie down and I hoped she would be sensible. It was sad that she felt so defeated by the prospect of leaving this doomed little bunch of benders.

7

I decided that I ought to contact some members of RAGE.
I wanted to find out whether they felt the women's peace
movement would be defeated by these final evictions.

I telephoned the public relations officer, Mr Learoyd. A girl
with a tremulous teenage voice answered.

'Can I speak to the spokesman of RAGE?' I asked her.

'He's at a RAGE meeting,' the girl said proudly. 'I'm the
spokesman of RAGE's daughter.'

'How long will your father be at the meeting?' I asked her.

She thought it would be a long time. I gave her the number
of the Newbury hotel where her father could reach me and
it was quite a long time before I heard from him.

I told Mr Learoyd that I would like to attend a RAGE
meeting, and asked him to tell me where they would be
holding the next one. He sounded a little horrified and
said that he would have to ask his chairman. RAGE didn't
have open meetings. Mr Learoyd hastily added that they
would be holding open meetings in the near future. He
seemed worried that I might get the impression there was
something sinister about the secrecy of his organization. He
told me that he would see what the chairman could do for
me.

The chairman telephoned me quite soon. He was afraid
he couldn't let me attend a meeting, but he would put me
in touch with 'the very best of RAGE'. He would give it
some thought as he only wanted me to meet the very best.
'I can assure you,' he said, 'I will only let you meet the very
best of RAGE.'

He seemed to have no idea how startling this sounded.

But later I received a message that said that he suggested I get in touch with a Mrs Scull. He had left me her number. The telephone operator in the hotel had written this woman's name as Mrs Skull.

Mr Learoyd telephoned me again that same evening. I asked him if he felt that the peace women would be defeated by the imminent evictions.

Like the antique dealer, he was certain that the evictions would never get rid of them. The antique dealer had been winkingly amused by the idea that the women would not be defeated by the new punitive move of the local council, but it made Mr Learoyd fulminate. He said I'd no idea how much damage those women were doing. I ought to see the filthy mess they had made on the Common. They were law-breakers. They danced naked. They were lesbians. They created health hazards. They smelt.

Enemies of the Greenham women always accused them of smelling. I was always waiting for the famous smell of the peace women, but I never once detected it on any of the camps. The camps smelt of wood smoke, but that was quite pleasant. The tanks that the women used as lavatories were deep in the woods and far away from the benders.

School children have always accused the new boy of smelling and the Greenham women were newcomers to Newbury, coming, as they did, from all over the British Isles and they were therefore threatening in the role of foreigners who had invaded a tight community. They had also introduced other foreigners in the shape of the Americans, the Australians, the Canadians, and Europeans.

After fulminating about the stink and the horror of the Greenham women, he told me that he had two daughters, that he had brought them up beautifully, that they were now responsible, decent members of the community.

I couldn't understand why he felt he had to tell a stranger about his beautifully brought-up daughters. Parents who make extravagant claims for the beautiful job they have done with their children always make me feel uneasy. But the spokesman of RAGE was most emphatic. His daughters were well-behaved and obedient. He was meandering off the point. But he was telling me something that he felt was very important. His daughters were not Greenham women.

He asked me if I'd seen the cartoon that RAGE had published in the Newbury *Weekly News*. I said that I hadn't seen it. I didn't feel like pretending that I admired it and as it obviously meant so much to him he would find a luke-warm response very rude. He said he'd like to come round to the hotel to show me a copy.

He came round with two versions of the RAGE caricature of the Greenham woman. The new cartoon had her looking just as hideous and still sitting astride the missile, but instead of carrying an olive branch, she was carrying a pair of wire-cutters.

Mr Learoyd was a much smaller, more dapper man than I'd expected. He was dark and thin-faced and pale. He said that the Greenham women had disappointed him. They had no sense of humour. He would have expected them to be able to laugh at the cartoons. But they had not.

Considering that the captions under the RAGE cartoons also exhorted the residents of Newbury to get rid of the Greenham squatters, he was asking for a lot of humour on the part of the women.

Mr Learoyd said that he was a newsagent – that he worked very hard – that the Greenham women were all lazy lay-abouts – that they were using their protest to do nothing. A lot of them were lesbians and they had only joined the camps in order to indulge in lesbian activity.

I didn't argue with Mr Learoyd. I wanted to hear his point of view. I soon felt that he'd turned the women's camps into a fantasy and he was tilting at windmills. The very laziest layabout could surely find much pleasanter places to enjoy idleness. Why would they choose those awful camps where it was necessary to work just to survive? As for the lesbians, there were so many comfortable lesbian clubs all over the British Isles. There were so many warm, pleasant places where the lesbians could be just as lesbian as they liked without any harassment. If they were only searching for some ideal place to pursue lesbian activities, they would have to be deranged to choose those awful camps where the battle against cold and hunger made any erotic feeling unimportant.

Mr Learoyd had the belief that the peace women were living it up in luxury on the perimeter. He said that I could have no idea how well those women lived. They were taking drugs – they were always drunk. The noise they made was unbearable for the Newbury residents.

Sometimes he liked to present the peace camps as stately pleasure domes of Xanadu. But then he would change his description without seeming aware of the contradictions, and he'd say that the peace women lived worse than any gypsies, that they only loved to wallow in squalor and filth.

I wondered if Mr Learoyd had visited any of the camps. He seemed as if he could make them just as he wanted.

When he endowed the women with fantastic wealth, he would shake with anger because their undeserved riches made him envious. When he presented them as dirty and poor, he hated them just as much. It was as if he felt that their poverty could somehow reduce him to rags and pull him down in the mud beside them.

I didn't tell him that I'd visited the camps. It interested me to hear how he would describe them to someone who had no idea of the facts.

He said that the Greenham women sent their children to school in taxis when everyone else's children had to use the bus. The taxis were paid for by the ratepayers.

These taxis made the Greenham women sound very extravagant. But I wondered if the school buses from Newbury had been prepared to go three miles out of their way in order to pick up children from the far gates of the perimeter.

In any case, there didn't seem to be any children on the peace camps at the moment. I'd seen only a couple of infants and they were much too young to require any transport to school. Mr Learoyd was furious that the Newbury ratepayers were spending so much on cab fares, but I couldn't believe that their bill was really very high.

Some of the peace women had tried to keep their children with them on the camps in the summer months, but Mr Learoyd said they'd had to be segregated from the Newbury school children in order to keep them safe.

'Like sex offenders in a prison?' I asked.

'Like sex offenders in a prison,' he said with satisfaction.

He told me that the children of the peace women had been so miserable at the local schools that they kept running away and going back to their mothers on the camps.

'They didn't like to feel unwanted. No one likes to feel that,' he said.

Mr Learoyd told me that his daughters loathed the Greenham women. If his daughters did something wrong he would threaten to send them off to the peace camps – they could think of no worse punishment.

'The peace camps have a very bad name in our household!' he said.

Mr Learoyd believed that every individual had a right to his views, but he was not going to put up with mob rule, and the Greenham women had introduced mob rule to Newbury. They broke the law on every possible occasion. They drove vehicles which had not passed their test for road worthiness. I imagined he must be talking about the battered old ambulances at Main Gate. They looked most unroadworthy, but I'd never seen them driven. They were used as stationary dwellings and they gave much more protection than the benders to any women who fell ill, and one of them was the home of the camp baby.

I found his attitude towards the Greenham women inexplicable. It was as if he felt there was no other evil in the world – that if he could only manage to get them off the Common, every other world problem would be solved.

Yet, he didn't live near to them. They didn't affect his newsagent's business. He said he'd put up a sign forbidding them from entering his shop. The women had many things to worry them, and I wondered if they really cared.

Mr Learoyd hoped that RAGE would be able to encourage more Newbury shopkeepers to refuse to serve them.

He found it unforgivable that they were attracting women from abroad. He'd heard that two bus-loads of women were coming over from Europe to support the women during their evictions.

'Now should they be allowed to do that?' he asked. 'Why should they be allowed to bring in those who can be termed as aliens?'

I'd read in the papers that some Dutch and Spanish women were soon expected to be arriving at Greenham. It was an archaic way to describe them.

'Why should they be allowed to bring in alien law-breakers?' he insisted. His organization was going to try and get the visas of these foreign women refused by the Home Office.

He was certain that if the Cruise missile was removed tomorrow the Greenham women would never leave – they'd just go on squatting on the Common. This was a highly unrealistic supposition, but it fitted in with both of his contradictory contentions. They would remain on the Common because they loved having no water since they hated washing. They would also be loathe to forgo all the luxury with which he insisted on endowing them.

'You ought to see the cars those women have got up there!' Mr Learoyd gave a whistle.

He made it sound as if Rolls Royces, Bentleys, and Cadillacs were parked outside the camps and yet it had seemed to me that lack of transport was the women's greatest problem.

'I certainly wouldn't mind owning the cars those women have got,' he said. He had forgotten he'd originally complained about the dreadful state of their unroadworthy vehicles.

It was quite late by then and he offered to drive me round the camps so that I could see how the women kept the local residents awake all night with their brawling. He wanted me to see the fire hazards they created by lighting fires in their sleeping benders. If they lit fires in those low, inflammable polythene constructions, I couldn't understand why so many were still alive, but I told him I'd be glad to be given a tour of the camps.

As we drove towards the perimeter, he told me that he would be frightened to walk on the Common at night.

'Do you really think the women might attack you?'

'I wouldn't walk at night on that Common. I certainly wouldn't like to walk past those women.'

The camps had never seemed so quiet. You wouldn't have known they were inhabited. Mr Learoyd was embarrassed by their deadness.

'They are not at it tonight,' he said.

He drove me round and round the base, always searching for a fire that had been lit in a sleeping bender. That night we couldn't find one.

The base always looked particularly sinister at night, with depressed-looking soldiers keeping lonely vigil in the watch towers. There were great stretches of perimeter that didn't seem to be guarded at all.

'Why is it so easy for the women to break into the base?' I asked Mr Learoyd.

'Take your most precious jewel,' he said. 'How can you defend it? If someone really wants to steal it, there's no way of keeping it safe. You would have to put it in a box with a bomb that would automatically blow up in the face of anyone who tried to open it.'

He was referring to the warheads as his most precious jewels.

He said that he'd like me to meet a Newbury housewife who loathed the peace women and he drove me to her house which was in a council block about half a mile away from the perimeter.

She was a big, fat, merry woman and she seemed very good-natured and on her breast she had a RAGE badge.

Mr Learoyd asked her to tell me how much she hated the peace women.

'I really loathe them,' she said. 'I see them as scum. Their habits are disgusting. You couldn't believe it.'

She loathed them because they used the public baths in

Newbury and they washed their filthy clothes in the public washing machines.

Mr Learoyd said he couldn't let his children use the Newbury swimming baths because the peace women used them. He said that the public baths now contained so much chlorine that if they were to put in any more it would be unsafe. That was all because of the Greenham women.

Mr Learoyd told me that two of the peace women had been invited to speak at his daughter's school. Her class had been doing a course on historical attitudes towards war and peace. His daughter had complained that one of the women had sat on the platform and breast-fed her baby in front of all the children. The other one had said she was proud to be lesbian.

If this lesbian note had been introduced in the school of Mr Learoyd's daughter, it seemed a mistaken move on the part of the peace women. A controversial issue had been raised which had no direct bearing on the subject that was meant to be under discussion.

The RAGE housewife told me that she was a socialist, whereas Mr Learoyd was a conservative. She only supported him on his attitude towards the Greenham women.

She had a friend in Newbury who had discovered that her teenage daughter was missing and she had asked the police to search the benders. They had refused because they were frightened of stirring up trouble in the camps. She found this outrageous when, as a ratepayer, she spent so much money on maintaining the police.

I asked if the teenager had really gone off to join the camps. Such a defection would have been unusual and therefore rather interesting. But the housewife's reply was disappointing. It appeared that the missing girl had turned up in a local disco.

It was still curious that the peace women seemed to be stirring up the ancient fear of the gypsies who were meant to come in the night and steal your children and take them away to live with them.

The rage that was expressed by the residents of Newbury was nearly always a very localised emotion. It focused on the way the ratepayer's money was spent or not spent.

I couldn't see why the police should be made to search the peace camps every time some Newbury mother went into panic because her teenager had gone off dancing. But the housewife felt that the Newbury police had betrayed their duties, that they were not repaying the ratepayers for the taxes they paid to finance them.

As Mr Learoyd drove me back to my hotel, he told me that when the Greenham women complained that pigs' blood had been thrown over them in the night – he couldn't feel much sympathy with them for they had thrown it over themselves.

I couldn't imagine them trudging off to some abattoir in order to obtain the blood that they would require for this self-defeating enterprise, but Mr Learoyd clearly saw them as capable of anything.

'You know something about those women,' he said. 'They hate the mud. They really hate the mud!'

Mr Learoyd told me that he couldn't forgive the way the women maltreated their babies by stripping them naked in freezing weather.

'Why would they do that?' I asked him. It sounded most uncharacteristic behaviour on the part of the women. I'd rarely seen a more beautifully cared-for and happy baby than the infant that had been born on Greenham Common. It was such a beaming, bouncing baby that it could have been used to advertise baby-food. Never once did I see any of the women deliberately strip it naked. The women doted on it. Few babies have had the love of quite so many women. As a lot of the women were separated from their children, it was sad to see the way they begged to 'borrow' it from its mother in order to cuddle and rock it. The Greenham baby seemed to be having an upbringing that would be the dream of child psychologists. Yet I'd been told that some of the Newbury social workers hoped to have it legally removed from its mother. The Greenham women said that these social workers didn't seem to realize that the baby's mother was herself a social worker.

Mr Learoyd told me that he had brought up his daughters to realize that they'd got to fit in with their parents. They had never been allowed to think that their parents were going to try to fit in with them. He loved his dog as much as he loved his daughters, but he'd taught his dog the same lesson. His dog had to fit in with him. He was not going to fit in with the ways of a dog.

When Mr Learoyd seemed to have forgotten about the Greenham women and he spoke of other matters, he was always still discussing them. This little story about the daughters and the dog was told to me as a warning. He was not a spokesman of RAGE for nothing. He was not a man who would fit in with Greenham women.

8

In the courthouse in Newbury, I attended the trial of the identical peace twins, Louisa and Ann Connell. They were both young peace campers and they looked identical so only their family could tell them apart.

A few weeks before, Ann Connell had been sent to Holloway for some offence to the perimeter. She had been released on condition she never returned within a twenty-five mile radius of the Cruise missile.

Ann Connell had very soon been picked up on Greenham Common and she'd been arrested on the charge of abusing her bail. It was then claimed that the police had picked up her identical twin sister, Louisa.

When the case was tried, the woman magistrate who found herself with the onerous task of judging a case without legal precedent, covered her confusion by carefully refusing to mention the defendant's name throughout the trial. When the clerk of the court called upon the defendant to take her place in the dock, he said, 'Call Ann Connell, if that is who she is.'

When the magistrate sentenced the twin to return to Holloway prison, she said, 'On the evidence before me I decide that you appear as Ann Connell.'

A policewoman had testified that she knew the defendant to be Ann Connell because of the length of her pointed incisor teeth. This little touch made Ann Connell sound dangerous and it represented one of the views that were widely held of the peace women – they were mad dogs with dangerous fangs and they might easily bite.

When I was at Main Gate, I'd been told that the policewoman had made a mistake when she had measured Ann Connell's incisor teeth – that Louisa was now in Holloway prison in the place of her sister. Louisa apparently didn't mind because she badly needed a rest from the camps and she'd been getting quite ill, and her twin was glad to let her have a break. Her lawyer, however, minded. She was troubled by this miscarriage of British justice. She had therefore asked for the twin who was currently imprisoned in Holloway to be released so that she could be identified by her brother in the Newbury courtroom.

The day that I went to the appeal of Louisa Connell, the brother of the twins had appeared for the identification. This unfortunate young man had been dragged away from his studies at Manchester University in order to sort out the muddle.

He'd come down on the train at his own expense and checked into a 'bed and breakfast' in Newbury. An innocent, and an outsider, he'd not realized that feelings ran very high in the town – that there was an ideological chasm separating the various groups in the town and that RAGE held great sway. In his naïvety, he had told the proprietor of his lodgings that his twin sisters were both peace protesters on Greenham Common.

The effect of this simple announcement had been electric. He'd been instantly kicked out of the 'bed and breakfast'.

It was a freezing night and it was late – provincial Newbury closes down very early and he didn't know where to go. He didn't feel he could ask to sleep in the peace camps where men were not allowed.

He tried to sleep on a bench in a bus shelter, but it started raining and without a blanket he had found sleep impossible. His situation was much worse than that of either of his twin sisters. Louisa was wrongly in Holloway, but at least she had a roof. Ann, who should have been in jail, at least had the fragile protection of her bender, and she had some kind of weak fire beside which she could huddle.

Finally, he made a desperate call to a resident of Newbury who had always been very kind to the peace campers. She was horrified to hear of his abysmal situation and she immediately invited him to stay the night in her warm and comfortable house. She also insisted on accompanying him to the trial when it took place the following day.

The trial of the identical twins very quickly took on a 'Mad Hatters' aspect, like many other things in Newbury. The Connell brother arrived in court looking tired and nervous.

The magistrate was a splendid John Bull of a man with a scarlet, shining bald-headed dome and imposing cotton-wool sideburns.

He asked Ann Connell to step forward to make her appeal and was told by her lawyer that she was unable to attend the court. He asked for an explanation and was told she was unable to attend because she was currently in jail. He had to accept this excuse, but the situation clearly made him feel bemused. Some form of breakdown of communications between the courts of Newbury and Holloway Prison had obviously occurred, and this didn't make it easy for him to administer justice. The brother of the twins had made his unpleasant trip in order to identify a missing sister, but there was little that anyone could do about it.

The magistrate then proceeded to try the case of five Mohican-headed peace campers who were accused of cutting a hole in the perimeter and entering the base.

The boredom of their trial was almost unbearable. They were being tried for an offence that had taken place many months ago. So many Greenham women were tried every day for similar offences that I wondered what happened to the unlucky regular criminals of Newbury. How did they ever get their cases heard?

The five young peace women with punk hair-styles were put in the dock and an English soldier from the missile base was asked to identify them by name. He looked more and more desperate as he was asked which of the girls was Jane and which was Mary. He was obviously not confident about his facts.

He stared at the Greenham women with despair. They

probably looked very much the same to him. They all had threatening haircuts. They were all trying to destroy everything he believed was best for England. He obviously found it painful to be asked to remember their individual names. His identifications were very faulty. He stumbled and made contradictions and errors. The young Greenham women laughed at him. The soldier got more and more flustered and he blushed.

The perimeter was then introduced as a theme and the whole case instantly became quite insufferably tedious. Where had the hole been cut? Could the soldier specify the precise area of the fence where criminal damage had been inflicted on it? He was handed a map. The defence lawyer for the women suggested that a map might refresh his memory. The soldier stared at it very despondently. The nine-mile perimeter fence is such a huge piece of wiring that when he was asked to pick out the exact spot on the map where it had been damaged, he had enormous and understandable difficulties.

The woman lawyer who represented the Greenham women was ruthless in her desire for precision. Had the wire of the fence been cut in the stretch that lay between Blue Gate and Indigo? Had it been cut between Turquoise and Orange?

The soldier continued miserably to consult the map, but it never seemed to help. The hole had been cut so long ago and since then innumerable holes had been cut in the perimeter and clearly all these different holes had fused in his mind.

But the lawyer wanted details of the particular hole that was taking up the court's attention. Could he give her some idea of its diameter? Had it been cut high or low on the fence? If it had been cut high, just how high had it been cut? If it had been cut low, could he specify just how low and tell the court in inches.

The soldier had obviously been much more interested by the sight of the Greenham women entering the base than by the hole they had cut in order to do so. He didn't seem to have paid much attention to their hole and his position was pitiful as he got vaguer and vaguer as he tried to recreate it.

The map of the perimeter was passed round and round the court. The prosecuting lawyer had to look at it. So did the lawyer for the defence. The soldier had to look at it again. Finally it was handed to the magistrate.

The unfortunate magistrate looked so depressed by the sight of this map that I wondered how many times in the last two years he had been made to look at it. It must be a dog's life for him, sitting all day in court and always having to look at this aerial recording of the perimeter.

'It's so important to get the details right,' he told the lawyers. I wondered if he really felt that. As the map circulated and recirculated round the court and the nature and location of the hole became less specific rather than more so, I wondered how the magistrate could bear to wake up in the morning, knowing he would have to spend the day focusing his attention on some damage that the perimeter had suffered.

Supposing that the magistrate was one of the prominent people in Newbury who secretly didn't care what happened to it, then his days would be even worse spent as he sat there listening to all this boring and often inaccurate testimony about offences which never varied in their nature. Lying in bed at night, this magistrate must sometimes start to see Greenham women cutting holes in the fence and entering the base. He could probably even start to count them as people count sheep going over stiles to fight off their insomnia.

'Considering the gravity of the charge ...' the lawyer of the peace women would say as she asked for another re-examination of the map in order to quibble over some minuscule point as to the exact placing of the hole on the perimeter.

The base is quite ill-lit at night and the soldier obviously hadn't been able to see the women very clearly and couldn't remember how many had entered on that one particular evening, or how many had nearly entered. He did his best.

But then another soldier was called in to give evidence and everything he said about the hole contradicted what the first soldier had said.

The precise location of the damage to the perimeter was once again called in question and the dreaded map had to be circulated once more and the magistrate was forced to take yet another look at it. The evidence of the second soldier also varied as to the number of women that he had seen entering the base on that far-off winter night.

I never got the impression that the soldiers were intentionally giving false evidence. When their statements sounded untrue, it came from the fallibility of the human memory rather than from the desire to divert the course of British justice.

I never heard how this case was resolved. As the testimony became increasingly tangled, there came a point when I could no longer bear to remain in the courtroom. I left the weary magistrate manfully battling on as he tried to establish which of the defendants had actually been carrying the criminal pair of wire-cutters. The lawyer was having her usual difficulties as she tried 'to refresh' the soldiers' memories.

9

While I was attending trials in the law courts of Newbury, the women of Blue Gate were evicted. When I next went back there, the benders had ceased to exist. It was hard to believe those squalid little colourful dwellings had ever been there. There was now only a lot of churned up mud, and the odd piece of newspaper and the odd trampled plastic spoon.

The perimeter now had an unsullied, unchallenged greyness. It looked triumphant and immovable as it reigned over the countryside with its rolling entanglements of barbed wire.

But although the camp had been wiped out, a little group of Greenham women were still there. They were sitting in a circle in the mud. As usual, it was bitterly cold.

They didn't speak very much. They just sat there as if they were having a make-believe picnic in mime. The food and the fire all had to be imagined. In reality, they now had nothing except mud.

The women always sat very quietly after any eviction. They behaved as if they had been winded and needed some time to recover their breath.

The hostility of the soldiers abated whenever one of the camps was destroyed. When the police and the bailiffs took on a cruel and punitive role, it was as if some kind of burden that compelled the military to ridicule and tease the women lifted. They became friendly towards them. They slipped them food from within the missile base and they sneaked them out cups of tea.

Once when a bailiff made a girl cry by seizing the plastic Ventolin inhaler that she used for her chronic asthma, the soldiers stood behind the perimeter as very stony-faced spectators and looked at him with disgust rather than approval. The Greenham women always became very distressed whenever photographs of their families were destroyed. They reacted with terror, as if they were the witnesses to a symbolic killing.

The day of the first eviction at Blue Gate, I was glad that Pat wasn't there. She had gone home to stay with her son.

One of the women told me that the bailiffs had been much more ruthless than they had been in the past. 'They mean business this time. They really mean to get us out,' she said.

Another woman said that the front-door keys of her house had been taken. 'It's such a boring nuisance. It means I'll have to get a new lock. That's going to cost me at least thirty quid.'

It was always surprising to be reminded that Greenham campers had anything as solid as houses, with front doors and locks. On the camps, you started to think that life on the Common was their only life.

Looking at the women sitting in a circle in the mud, it seemed as if these new evictions would be the end of their protest. How could they remain by the base without a piece of bread or a drop of water? All their water-containers had been confiscated. How would they survive without any form of shelter once night fell?

'The bailiffs didn't hurt us,' one of them said to me. 'But the eviction was violent. You feel violated if your things are pulled out of your hand. That kind of violation has to seem violent.'

As they sat round in a circle in the mud, they seemed to be waiting for something miraculous to happen. It was difficult to see what that could be. Their situation looked hopeless. They appeared to be waiting for manna to drop from heaven.

But then, in a sense, it did start to drop. Slowly a great trickling army of supporters began to arrive. Well-dressed married couples drove up in their cars, as though coming to relieve the siege of Mafeking.

They had brought their children who were all carrying firewood, water-containers, bread and coffee for the women. Many of them came from Newbury. Later came the ones who had driven all the way down from Scotland, the ones who had come from Wales. They had all heard of the Greenham evictions on the radio.

They made efficient lists of the camp requirements, and they drove off to Newbury to pick up the various items – eggs, salt, washing-up liquid, flour. The normality of the typical housewife's list was odd in view of the peculiar situation at Blue Gate.

As the whole position of the Greenham women was a symbolic one, they sometimes seemed like the high-priestesses of a mysterious cult who required more esoteric symbolic offerings than toothpaste, soap, and Brillo pads for their washing-up.

When male supporters of the Greenham women arrived with various gifts, many of them were very shy and awkward. At first, they didn't dare to give their presents to the peace campers. They were ignorant of the protocol of the camps. Were they allowed to go up to the women who were sitting in a circle in the mud? Could they just hand them bags of potatoes and packets of fire-lighters or could these gifts only be relayed to the women through some female intermediary?

They kept a distance, looking embarrassed and clutching sets of plastic spoons and sheets of polythene. It was as if they believed that there was an invisible and magical ring surrounding the Greenham women which no male could pass with impunity.

Once they grasped that the women would not be offended if they went right up to them and handed them their offerings, they looked relieved and proud as if they'd passed some gruelling test.

'Don't thank me – you are doing all the work,' I heard a young man say as he bashfully handed one of the women a ten-pound note.

'Do you know that a guy has just given us fifty Gortex bags!' a peace camper said to me. 'Isn't that fantastic! I think we'll be all right now. I think we will get through the night.'

A women lit a fire and with its first puff of feeble smoke the dead camp seemed to come alive again.

By the end of the day they had made new benders which seemed to have sprung up from the earth like mushrooms. The food supplies at Blue Gate were better than they had ever been. The women had wine and whisky. Mr Learoyd would have been horrified by all the luxury.

The women put up a placard outside their newly resurrected camp. Their sign said 'Business as Usual'.

The night that the women of Blue Gate suffered their first eviction, a missile carrier came past them out of the base and did a practice run through the countryside.

I read in a newspaper that a Mrs Scull had leaned out of her bedroom window in her nightdress and cheered as she saw the carrier of the warheads. I then realized she must be the owner of the red-brick house that was just across the road from the camp at Blue Gate. Until then, I'd not realized that the camp was overlooked by the woman who had been described to me as 'the very best of RAGE'.

The press reported the event as a triumph of the military over the peace women. 'Greenham women caught napping' read the headlines. Blue Gate was described as 'heavily guarded' by the Greenham women and the success of the military over the peace protestors was so gloatingly dwelt upon that it was made to sound as if Britain had defeated the Russians.

There had only been twelve women on the camp at Blue Gate that night. They had been cordoned off by such a huge ring of police that they had been powerless to do anything.

'What did you do when you saw the carrier coming out of the base?' I asked them.

'We wept,' I was told. 'What else could we do?'

The military claimed that the carrier had not been transporting live warheads.

'How do we know?' the women asked me. 'And how do the Russians know?'

They said that the sight of the vast carrier emerging from the base had made them shake. Their shaking had continued long after it was out of sight. They felt traumatized by having witnessed a manoeuvre that they saw as part of the practice for the holocaust.

They had been horrified by Mrs Scull when she had leaned from her window and cheered the missile carrier. 'She behaved like a real barmy Beatrice.'

The women said they had seen some other very nasty games being played in the base in the night. A green flag would be put up and a siren would go. This was all practice for the 'Red Alert'. Once the siren wailed, the American wives and children were rushed from their military quarters close to Newbury. They had to be hurried into the nuclear bunkers within the base.

'I think those exercises are so cruel to the American children,' a peace camper said. 'Those poor little kids look really terrified. They hear the siren and then they are dragged out of bed. They look white. You see them all crying as they are rushed by coach to the bunkers. They are still in their night clothes. They don't believe it's only practice. They think the end has come.'

The women told me that the British police never looked too happy as they had to wave the Americans in through the gates. They had no bunkers, and the exercise reminded them that in a war they would be left for dead.

Once the military were all in symbolic safety in their nuclear shelters, a black flag was always flown on the base.

'It's so stupid, and wicked, that black flag,' one of the peace women said. 'On the great day, who do they think will be around to fly any black flags!'

The Greenham women often asked the British police what they thought of 'Red Alert'. They always became sheepish and told her it wasn't their exercise.

'It certainly isn't their exercise,' the Greenham women said.

*

When I tried to telephone Mrs Scull to find out if she was pleased or disappointed by the evictions of the peace women, I was told by her husband that she was attending a RAGE meeting and she would be there for most of the day.

Mrs Scull and Mr Learoyd seemed to spend so much time at these meetings. I wondered if their discussions took on the choleric nature that the name of their organization suggested and this slowed them down.

When I finally reached Mrs Scull, she said that the people of Newbury were suffering horribly from the mob rule of the Greenham women. She said she would be glad to show me what they had done to her view and I could have no idea what they'd done to the value of her house. It broke her heart.

She sounded distraught. Yet I found her view indescribably ugly without the camps. If they were to be removed for ever, while the base remained, her view could never be much improved. But Mrs Scull seemed to be able to blot out the sight of the vast military installation that was right in front of her windows. She appeared to see only a lovely and peaceful English common which had been ruined by the benders of the peace campers.

After speaking to her, I decided to check with a house agent in Newbury. I was curious to find out how much the Greenham women had affected the value of houses that faced the perimeter. So many myths sprung up around the women that it was difficult to separate fiction from reality.

I told the house agent that I was enquiring about local properties on behalf of my daughter who was anxious to buy a house that looked on to the perimeter. I thought he might find such a daughter very weird in her tastes, but he found her desires normal for she could apparently get a house, if it was sited on the perimeter, at least £5,000 cheaper than if she was not exposed to the Greenham women.

'They've done a lot of damage to the value of properties round the base,' he told me.

I asked if the missile base itself had affected the value of houses that faced it.

'Oh, no. The base has never affected property values. It's only the women. The base has never done a thing to property values – why should it?' He said that he unfortunately didn't have a house that directly faced the Cruise missile.

'Does you daughter really insist on facing the perimeter?' he asked. 'I have some nice houses that are very near the base – but they don't quite face it – and they are not really all that near to the Greenham women.'

The conversation was starting to become absurd. My daughter was sounding madder by the minute as she insisted on facing a barbed-wire vista very similar to that of a concentration camp in order to get her property reduction.

I hastily told the house agent that she really insisted on facing the perimeter in order to prevent him from telling me the details of all the other houses that he had on his lists. I was glad of this excuse for it allowed me to get out of his office.

In the main street of Newbury, there was a group of young Dutch women who were passing out little bits of cheese on sticks and also peace pamphlets to the people of Newbury. I realized that this little group of blonde students must be part of the bus-loads from Holland that Mr Learoyd wanted the British Home Office to forbid from entering the country.

As the Dutch peace protesters handed out their literature, youths from Newbury came up to them with their faces red and twisted with anger. They grabbed their bits of cheese and stamped them into the ground. They stamped and stamped on the cheese. Their stamping looked maniacal. Their anger, as they destroyed these harmless bits of cheese, had got out of all proportion. The cheese stuck to their soles and this enraged them further. They tried furiously to scrape it off. But they had ground it so deep into their boots that it was not easy to remove.

The Dutch girls went very white. They looked baffled and terrified. They seemed unprepared for the malevolence of this attack. Unlike the women of Greenham Common, they were clearly unaccustomed to a peace protest arousing such strong feelings of aggression.

They stood there in the main street of Newbury and watched in disbelief as the loutish youths came up and grabbed their pacifist pamphlets and tore them into such tiny pieces they reduced them to confetti.

The Dutch women were very neat and tidy and they had not been sleeping out rough on the Common for many months. The Greenham women were reputed to stir up hostility because they looked unkempt and sluttish, but seeing how much the Newbury youths hated the neat Dutch students, their neatness obviously made no difference. They were still loathed because they had no enthusiasm for the destructive powers of nuclear missiles.

The Newbury hooligans were not conspicuous for their bravery and they liked to attack those who were unable to retaliate. They loathed the sight of an American military uniform almost as much as they loathed the sight of a peace pamphlet. They made it so unpleasant for the US soldiers when they came into the local pubs that many of them couldn't face going out for a drink in Newbury. The town was not a sparkling centre of entertainment and the American soldiers defending the base had a much more excruciatingly boring time than the British. As the youths tormented them if they went into the pubs, their evenings were deadly for they found there was nothing to do.

The politics of the hooligans were mindless and they could be adjusted to any given situation. They only approved of the Cruise missile if the Greenham women opposed it. They disliked it when the US military came into the local pubs because they viewed their uniforms as those of an occupying army. Their feelings of patriotism, which expressed themselves in the Union Jacks which they sewed on their black leather studded sadists' costumes, were jarred by the sight of American uniforms because it reminded them that Britain had no Cruise missiles of her own, and she had no say in the deployment of the one she housed on the Common.

The youths knew that the very uniform that had all the power made the Americans their victims within the local situation. They could taunt and jeer at the US military with impunity. They could cast the most sneering aspersions on their masculinity. The Americans were under orders not to tangle with civilians. They were not meant to get into fights and inflame the resentment that many British people felt about the presence of the US missile.

If the American soldiers could only have got together with the Greenham women, they would have found a great bond in their mutual dislike of the stupid floating aggression of the local youths. On the perimeter, such a conciliation was most unlikely.

10

The eviction of the camp at Blue Gate was only the first of a series of evictions on the perimeter. After that the bailiffs came round every day and they systematically destroyed every camp on the base, with the exception of Main Gate which was due to be destroyed under a different, more ominous legal order, 'road-widening'.

The Greenham women became much less distressed by the evictions – once they became so frequent they became monotonous. Some of them went into Gortex survival bags and no longer bothered to rebuild their benders after they had been demolished.

A girl at Blue Gate told me that she had suffered from violent claustrophobia when she'd spent her first night in a Gortex. The survival bags had fluorescent zips on the inside and you were meant to pull them when you wanted to get out. She'd been unable to find her zip despite its fluorescence and she'd gone into a state of panic in the cold dark bag, feeling that she had been buried alive. She'd never before felt so terrified by the vandals from Newbury. She loathed the idea that if they came creeping up on her she wouldn't be able to see them coming.

In the day-time, the women went hopping round the ruins of their annihilated camps wearing their Gortexes unzipped like children in a sack race. They were so valuable and expensive, these bags, that they didn't dare to take them off because the bailiffs could take all possessions that were not attached to their persons.

As the evictions relentlessly continued the camps attracted more and more supporters. In Newbury, the residents who sympathized with the women developed a system by which they adopted a camp. Blue and Indigo, Turquoise and Violet became their orphans and however viciously the camps were eradicated, the women still had bread and water and firewood by night-time.

Their food supplies had to be kept down to the barest minimum, for the bailiffs sometimes evicted the camps twice a day and if they became over-stocked it was wasteful.

The camp at Blue Gate seemed to be particularly resilient and, however often it was razed to the ground, by evening Mrs Scull's view was as bad as ever.

The weather got a little better and a few daffodils came out near the camps. They didn't look cheering, they looked depressing as they came up round the perimeter. They seemed doomed. If there was some accident within the base, those flowers would never grow again.

When the children of the Greenham women came down to visit their mothers, they picked the daffodils and stuck them in the steel loops of the perimeter.

I saw an enraged paratrooper rushing towards a little girl who was decorating the fence. He was snarling and making furious baboon faces to frighten her. She remained very cool. She wasn't frightened. 'How old are you?' she asked him.

The visiting children would also blow up balloons and tie them to the fence. There wasn't much for them to do on the camps. It was as boring for them as it was for the peace women. Their only important activity was the protest of their presence.

I watched a pompous and elderly rider in a bowler hat jog past one of the camps as he exercised his chestnut mare on what was left of Greenham Common. When he saw the balloons, he rode up to the perimeter in a rage. One by one, he methodically popped all the balloons with his riding-stick. There was great anger round the base, but it often found very petty expression.

I saw another man from Newbury walking past Blue Gate. He was exercising his dog, and he had it on a lead. There was a camp dog at Blue Gate and the dog of the passing man got very excited and tried to run to greet it. Its owner was so horrified that his dog should be trying to fraternize with an animal that belonged to the Greenham women that he tightened his grip on its lead. He lifted it up in the air so that it was dangling in space and choking pitifully as its collar bit into its neck.

'You bloody stupid women!' he shouted at the camp. He was most probably a dog-lover and he was being cruel to his pet in order to be kind. He didn't want to let it catch the disease that he felt the camp dog would give it.

'How can he do that to an animal?' one of the campers asked as she watched him swinging his heavy dog as if he wanted to use it as a weapon to clout the women. 'Sometimes everything seems really hopeless,' she said.

One day a couple of very old ladies came tottering past Mrs Scull's house as they took their evening stroll. They were wearing such old-fashioned tweed suits and buttoned-up boots – they seemed to be part of an England of a long-lost age.

I wondered what these ancient figures would think of the Greenham women, and I went up to them and asked them. They felt exactly like Mrs Scull. 'It's a crime what these women are doing to this Common. And it's such a beautiful spot. Don't you think it's a beautiful spot? But have you ever seen such an eyesore as those camps? It's really disgusting and the evictions don't seem to be working at all.'

It always surprised me when the residents of Newbury said that they still found their Common beautiful. It was as if they continued to see it as it once had been.

The two old ladies pointed to the peace camp and without seeming to see it, to the perimeter fence. 'It's really a crime what those women are doing to our Common,' they repeated.

In high, quavery, indignant voices they complained about their rates. The Greenham women were costing a fortune. The women kept damaging the perimeter and every time that it had to be repaired, it all came out of the taxpayers' money.

'Mind you, I don't know how those women manage to

exist,' one of the old ladies said with a certain admiration. 'Just look at the state of that camp. How do they do it? It's really incredible.' They both started grumbling again about their rates. The women needed so much policing and that all cost money.

'We've got to have nuclear weapons,' one of them said. 'All the experts say we have to have them. But we certainly don't want another war. We have lived through three wars already.'

I didn't know which third war they were referring to. They seemed resolutely English in their attitudes and I felt only English wars would mean very much to them. Incredibly old as they looked, surely they couldn't mean the Boer War? Could old age have befuddled them so they miscounted the wars that they had actually experienced? Could they already have lived through a nuclear war in some buried and terrified part of their imagination? There had suddenly been a look of real terror in their wizened little old faces when they told me they didn't want another war. Just for one moment they had both looked beyond the camp of the peace women and they had stared at all the military activity that was going on within the base. Then they turned away as if they couldn't bear the sight of it and they went hobbling off to continue their stroll round the Common.

Immediately after they left, another elderly upper-class couple walked down the road that separated Mrs Scull's house from the camp that she so hated. There was a husband wearing a Sherlock Holmes tweed cap. He had the fierce white handlebar moustache of the English colonel. There was a wife with a face as round and rosy as a plum and she was wearing a long tweed cape.

The couple looked extremely staid and conventional and I assumed they must feel very strongly about their rates, that they would be disgusted by the Greenham women. I decided to ask them what they felt about the evictions and was surprised that they took a very different view from the ancient ladies.

The wife immediately became very heated about the rates she was paying. She couldn't bear having to finance the evictions.

'It's costing us a fortune to evict those women. All those police, all those bailiffs, it's quite ridiculous! And it doesn't even work.' She pointed to some of the peace women who were struggling with a sheet of polythene as they started to make a brand new bender.

She said that she found the missile base the real eyesore, not the camps. 'Those camps could be cleared up in a second. I don't understand the people who make a fuss about the look of the camp. You have a huge rotting carcass on your doorstep and then you start complaining about the flies. It makes me despair. How can people be so stupid!'

She said she wanted to cry everytime that she looked at the Common. 'It used to be all gorse and silver birches and wild flowers and heather. Just look at it now.' She gave a shiver. 'It's not even legal to seize common land. But no one cared about that and none of us got any compensation.'

She asked me if I'd noticed the condition of the streets in Newbury. 'You couldn't have a worse hazard for an old pair of legs.'

She said that the reason that the Newbury streets were in such a terrible state was that no one repaired them because they were too busy spending the ratepayers' money on policing the Greenham women.

'Do you know how much they spent on extra-policing for those women last year? Over three million pounds! Those women don't need such hoards of police. It's absurd. It's really wicked!'

She said it was very hard to find a policeman in Newbury any more. 'They've got them all down on the Common policing those unfortunate women.'

She said that she didn't feel safe when she was walking to a whist party in the evenings. She lived in fear. The Newbury youths were mugging old people left, right and centre.

It was grotesque that the dreaded Newbury youths seemed

to be benefiting so richly from the situation on Greenham Common. They had a wealth of brutal ways to spend their evenings. They could mug the old Newbury ladies as they went tottering off to their whist parties. They could torment the American soldiers in the pubs, and when they got bored with that they could always whip up some pigs' blood and throw it at the Greenham women.

The rosy-faced lady pointed at Mrs Scull's house. 'Did you read about that woman leaning out of her window in her nightie and cheering the missile convoy? I find that much worse than anything the peace women do. I found it really shaming!'

I wasn't quite certain whether she minded Mrs Scull exposing herself publicly in her nightie or if it was her enthusiastic greeting of the warheads that she found so deeply shocking.

Her military-looking husband kept nodding as she complained about the nightie. When she said she found it obscene, he violently agreed with her.

'When we were young we used to think it would be awful to grow old,' his wife said to me. 'But now we are glad to be old. It means we don't have much longer. What a mess we have all made of it! What a world we have made for ourselves! Oh, yes, we are certainly glad to be old. We might even die a natural death.'

She pointed at the new bender that was being constructed by the campers. 'Those women are not so stupid. You can say what you like about them. But they know what's going to happen to us all. Don't you think that women always know these things? Don't you think that women are always more far-sighted?'

The tenacity of the Greenham women seemed more and more extraordinary as they entered this new phase of their protest and had to survive the twice-a-day evictions. They got even less sleep, for the police came round all through the night and put out their fires with hydrants.

One night I was driving round the base and I discovered the camp at Indigo in the most forlorn condition. It had only two girls keeping watch on the perimeter. They had neither Gortex bags nor benders and they were lying on the side of the road wrapped in blankets. The police had just put out their fire and confiscated their firewood. They had also lost their candles and they were lying there in the dark.

I stopped and asked them if I could bring them anything. Firewood was obviously what they needed most. It had been raining all day and the woods were much too wet to be able to provide fuel and I couldn't think where I could get them firewood at two o'clock in the morning.

The girls said they were all right. They thought they could get through the night. Tomorrow they were going to Iceland. If I was around tomorrow, they would be grateful if I'd give them a lift to Main Gate. They wanted to say goodbye to the women there before they left.

The Greenham women were internationally very famous and their fares were paid and they were flown all over the world so they could address peace meetings, and it was ironic that it was almost easier for them to get to Iceland than to get to the camp at Main Gate.

It seemed so dangerous, what these two girls at Indigo were doing. It was eerily isolated and dark on that part of the perimeter. I felt that anything could happen to them as they lay there on the roadside. They were at the mercy of any rapist or lunatic.

I'd been told that the mothers of the young peace campers became hysterical with worry as they thought of their daughters sleeping out on a public road. Finding these girls lying there alone in the dark at Indigo, I could see that their mothers might become deranged with anxiety, if they saw their situation.

One of the girls was Irish and she said that she was starting to feel very homesick. She was longing to go back to see her family. But after Iceland, she would have to come back to Newbury for she had a charge coming up.

I asked her what charge she was facing.

'Wilful damage to a policeman's shoe.'

'Did you wilfully damage his shoe?'

'No, I certainly didn't!' she said indignantly. 'I was paint-ing a peace symbol on a military truck, and this clumsy idiot knocked over my paint and put his foot in it.'

She said she would plead guilty to the painting of the truck, but she was going to fight the wilful damage to the shoe.

Poor magistrate with the fluffy sideburns. I thought of him with sympathy. This was going to be the most deadly case for him. Presumably the incident had taken place very close to the perimeter. There would be the dreaded map again and the exact relationship of the shoe to the paint – the paint to the fence of the base.

'Considering the gravity of the charge, your honour ... the Greenham women's lawyer would say as she asked for more and more witnesses to be called. The magistrate would have to listen to all their hesitant and lengthy testimony and he'd have to examine the damaged object. A smelly and unattractive shoe would have to be passed round and round the court from the defence lawyer, to the prosecuting lawyer, to the Irish girl, to the policeman and then back to his Honour.

The testimony of the witnesses under oath might very easily turn out to be unreliable in which case the Irish girl's lawyer would appeal and the whole case would have to be tried anew.

After the magistrate had heard enough about this wretched shoe, he might start to wish he was listening to one of his more routine cases in which blushing, uncertain soldiers tried to recreate holes they had found on the perimeter.

'The British police inside the base are so funny,' the Irish girl said to me. 'They can be so horrible to us and then they'll suddenly come and chat. They tell us how much they hate the food they are given by the Americans. I suppose we are the only women around for them, and men like to have women to grumble to. But when they try and turn us into mother figures, we really find it a bit much. They can see what the police have done to our camps. They can see what they've done to our fires. They can see that we haven't got a scrap to eat. And yet they still seem to need our breasts to lean on. They come and grumble to us through the perimeter fence and they have the nerve to complain about the American food!'

I finally went to visit Mrs Scull in order to look at the
frightful things that had been done to her view. She was a
middle-aged woman with bright buttercup hair. I thought
she looked very tired. I wondered whether the long hours
she had spent attending the RAGE sessions had exhausted
her. Maybe she had hoped for too much from the evictions
and every time she now saw a new bender springing up in
the camp in front of her house she had much the same
sickening feeling of helplessness that the peace women felt
when they saw the missile carrier go out cruising through
the English countryside.

'I read in the newspapers that you cheered the military
convoy,' I said to Mrs Scull.

She looked rather cross and unwelcoming and I thought
some recognition of her current fame might please her.

'I most certainly did. It was a defeat for those women.'

I found myself trying to picture Mrs Scull as she had
looked as she leant from her window in her nightie. I didn't
mind the nightie like the woman in the tweed cape had
minded it. At least Mrs Scull had been untroubled by the
niceties of conventional behaviour as she gave full vent to
her emotions. It had been an act of bravura when she had
thrown caution to the winds and screamed hip hooray to
the carrier of the warheads. Publicly displaying herself in
her nightie, she had been courageous in her impetuous and
reckless disregard of public opinion. She had been prepared
to expose herself, body and soul, without thought to the
consequences. She had been so very bold in her expression of
all her inner feelings that she had been untrammelled by any

of the small town pettiness that could often seem the blight of Newbury.

From the perspective of Mrs Scull's stockbroker ancient-style house, her view was certainly appalling. The camp at Blue Gate really looked a mess and it had been made to look much worse than it had once used to look, by the bailiffs. When the benders had stood there as dwellings, they had never been objects of architectural beauty, but they once had some life and they once had character.

Now they were only the remnants of benders, they had none of the dignity of the ancient ruin. They had become merely torn sheets of muddy polythene. The sticks that had once been their foundations lay scattered all over the site with the odd kettle and cup that had been overlooked in the purges.

'I could weep when I look at that,' Mrs Scull said.

The perimeter itself looked atrocious that day. It was covered with ripped pieces of darning wool and daffodils that had died in its looped wire. It was decorated, with popped balloons which had the sordid look of scarlet and yellow dangling contraceptives. Mrs Scull didn't seem to be able to see the fence. She saw only the women trying to get a fire going.

'This used to be such a beautiful spot,' Mrs Scull said. 'We were so happy here.' She seemed close to tears. She was pitiful.

She said that she was selling her house although she loved it. She was not going to subject herself to the mob rule of the Greenham women. 'They have lesbians in their camps.' She gave a shudder.

She took me up to her bedroom. The camp looked rather unimportant from a higher perspective. Mrs Scull had a really fantastic view of the desolation of the missile base. From her window, you could see much more barbed wire than you could see from the ground. It seemed to roll out to infinity.

She asked me to imagine how pretty her view had been before the women had set up their camp. She saw that I was taken aback by her uninterrupted vista of military vehicles and barbed wire. She blamed the barbed wire on the Greenham women. It had never been there before they arrived. She seemed to feel that if the Greenham women would only vanish, all the hideous defences of the base would vanish. Did she think that warheads could be housed without protection, like flowers on a common?

She said she could never forgive the Greenham women for what they had done to the wild life in the area. She was a passionate bird-lover and she said that there had once been some very rare birds on the Common, but they had stopped nesting there because of the women.

'What rare birds used to nest here?' I asked her.

Apparently Greenham Common had once been the habitat of the Pied Fly Catcher and the Little Ringed Plover. I couldn't help thinking that Mrs Scull was projecting some of her own fastidious feelings onto these rare birds. Surely the Pied Fly Catcher and the Little Ringed Plover wouldn't be so distressed by the unaesthetic appearance of the camps that they would refuse to nest in their vicinity. They might even quite like the Greenham women, for there were always crumbs on their camps. There was also the possibility that all the lights that flashed in the night in the base, all the noise of helicopters and juggernauts, had driven this rare species from the Common. If they had any sense, they would fly from a spot that was so unconducive to peaceful nesting.

Mrs Scull said that she had an appointment and she couldn't give me any more of her time. I assumed that she was going off to a RAGE meeting.

In the hotel bar in Newbury, England seemed a much safer place to be than it seemed when one was down on the perimeter. Down on the base, it was impossible to ignore the threat of the nuclear weapons that were lurking like invisible sharks within the silos.

The stillness of the missile was sinister and so was its silence. The missile seemed all the more powerful because it had no need to make the constant din of the military. As the military went buzzing around in their helicopters, their farting motor bikes, their groaning articulated lorries, they seemed as feeble as toy soldiers compared to their own hidden weapons. They were made to appear childish by the missile with its terrifying and dignified silence. Was all their noisiness only a way of denying their powerlessness? The defenders of the base only appeared strong when they were tough with the Greenham women.

Down on the camps by the perimeter all the doubts that had been cast on the missile by its various detractors became much more nagging. The American manufacturers who supplied the warheads were not threatened by the possibility of law-suits as they were in the United States. They could supply the Europeans faulty nuclear equipment without fear of redress. What would happen if they were to do this?

The 'hardware' of the missile is subject to corrosion through fatigue and wear and bad design. Senator John Warner, who conducted the US hearings on the safety of handling nuclear and chemical weapons, said to some senior military officers, 'Gentlemen, I presume that your stock piles in Europe are suffering some of the same decomposition problems.' General Fulwyler made a reply to the senator and his answer was deleted from the record. Down on the perimeter, this deletion didn't seem reassuring.

What were the real risks of a nuclear accident? What were the risks of what the Newbury papers called the 'civic catastrophe'? The local authorities were asking for volunteers whom they could train in order to combat this emergency. Did they feel it was inevitable?

All the possibilities of error seemed very real when one was in the camps of the peace women. Human error, error of computer and machinery, any error that could occur with something as deadly as plutonium could bring about the most appalling casualties.

In the bar of the hotel in Newbury, the beer mugs hung shining from a rack. There were bridles on the walls. There were sporting prints of huntsmen and jockeys. All seemed quite well with England.

The three miles that separated one from the base gave the illusion that one was out of the range of the dangers of the missile. The nearer one got to it, the more one was aware of its dangers.

It was not very realistic to feel protected by a three-mile separation from the perimeter – not if one remembered the huge areas of Great Britain that had become automatic enemy targets since the arrival of nuclear weapons and power stations.

But in the hotel it was easier to go to sleep in the snow – like the peace women's doomed Arctic explorer, and Mrs Scull's apparent inability to see the perimeter fence seemed perfectly understandable. She had to live with that fence and she had found a way to deal with the misgivings it must sometimes arouse in her. She had moved her attention away from it and feared only the mob rule of the Greenham women.

In the Newbury bar, one felt safer than on Greenham Common because no one mentioned Jerry Falwell's pamphlet in which he reassured Born Again Christians that they need not worry about nuclear war or Armageddon because they would all go up in 'rapture' before it occurred. They would be driving their automobiles and they would hear the trumpet sound and up they would go to Jesus, leaving all the unchristian passengers in their cars, first to crash, and then to go into a period of Tribulation which would end with Armageddon.

It was doubtful that many of the people frequenting the Newbury hotel had even heard of Jerry Falwell or knew that he represented the immensely powerful American Moral Majority. They discussed business affairs and racing results but no one ever said that they found it frightening that Jerry Falwell claimed Ronald Reagan was a 'Born Again Christian'. They expressed no anxiety that an American president who felt he was going to be automatically 'raptured' might view nuclear war with a certain nonchalance.

When I was having a drink in the hotel in the evening I met a young man who had his own form of 'Born Again' attitudes towards the holocaust.

He was drinking beer with an older man and I was invited to join them.

In Newbury, it was never very long before the conversation turned to the evictions of the Greenham women. The subject of rates also came up there more quickly than in most English towns, and people very soon spoke of death. The young man, who looked baby-faced and fresh, said that he saw the peace women as a bloody nuisance. The older man thought their principles were right, but they were going about their protest the wrong way. He felt he was lucky to be a Newburian because the town would be a direct hit in the event of a war. He would be killed outright and that's what he would choose.

The younger man said that he didn't feel like that at all. He didn't think Newburians were lucky. He would like to be a nuclear survivor.

'Why do you want to be a nuclear survivor?' I asked him.

'I think it would be a challenge,' he said.

Only that day I'd read a grim book while I was on the base with the peace campers. It was written by two doctors and it was entitled *The Medical Consequences of Nuclear Weapons*. In their matter-of-fact, scientific prose they warned how little they would be able to do for any nuclear survivors. They reminded the public of the incalculable number of doctors and nurses who would be killed or be suffering from multiple injuries, radiation burns and blindness. The hospitals would be demolished. Any surviving doctors would have no pain-killers, antibiotics, or blood for transfusions. Thousands of people would be trapped in the masonry of buildings and would die in agony without medical aid. In the inferno there would be no one to rescue them.

This book painted a picture of hell as it prophesized the panic that survivors would experience as they staggered round with their flash-burns, vomiting incessantly from radiation sickness and searching for the children and relatives that they had lost.

When the young man told me that he thought it would be a challenge to be a survivor, I remembered one of the most gruesome and horrific warnings in the medical book.

The doctors said that the human eye melts when exposed to the fireball. In Hiroshima, survivors were found with eyes that were running down their cheeks like tears.

'I don't understand why you want the challenge of being a survivor,' I said to the young man.

In his schoolboy fantasy, he pictured himself in a Robinson Crusoe situation with a few other nuclear survivors. He thought it could all be very jolly and challenging as they had their various adventures on a poisoned planet. He felt invigorated by the idea of starting humanity anew.

To this young man, the Greenham women were bound to seem a bloody nuisance since they were trying to prevent him from having an adventurous exciting future. His attitude towards the possibility of the holocaust was 'Born Again' in the sense that he saw it as something that it was possible to survive, miraculously unscathed.

It was only when he remembered how near he lived to the perimeter that ugly reality intruded upon his pipe-dream. However much he would have liked to delude himself, he couldn't visualize there being many people who would have a 'fun-time' after surviving the destruction of Newbury.

His vision was very different to that of the peace women. Where this young man saw challenge, they saw only blood, burnt, peeling skin, and melting eyeballs. It was terror of their own vision which had compelled them to become a bloody nuisance on Greenham Common.

'Those women had a real defeat when they couldn't stop the missile carrier coming out of the base,' the young man said to me. 'They can't beat the military. So they might as well admit it. They might as well all pack up and go home.'

He spoke of the Greenham women as if they were a huge armed force who *might* have beaten the military. If the peace women had any force at all, it was obviously only a moral force. When he showed his contempt for their defeat, he was unconsciously ascribing to them powers that they had never pretended to possess, and by doing so he gave them a tribute without realizing it. He was recognizing that a moral force can be something to be reckoned with.

12

The eviction of the peace women at Main Gate was the most symbolically important of all the evictions that took place around the base. Main Gate had the oldest camp on the perimeter. It was to this gate that women had marched from Wales in 1981 and had set up their first camps and declared that they refused to leave until the whole issue of housing American weapons on British soil was aired in a public debate.

The 'road-widening' scheme under which the camps at Main Gate were doomed to destruction represented a much more serious attempt to wipe out the protest of the women than the ones that had been made on the other camps. At Main Gate the ground was destined to be literally torn from under the peace women's feet.

One morning I went there to see if the 'road widening' had started and a sordid little incident occurred which seemed unpleasantly typical of life on the perimeter.

I was accompanied that day by two girls who had also come down from London. We parked on the right side of the Main Gate and got out of the car. The camp had still not been destroyed and the peace women were all sitting round their fire on the other side of the lane that leads out of the base.

We were just going to cross this lane when a coach-load of soldiers emerged from the base and we waited on the side of the slip-road in order to allow the bus to pass.

As it came past us, every window in the coach suddenly filled up with something huge and threatening and white. The soldiers had taken down their trousers while still within the base and when they saw us standing on the side of the road, they put themselves into an ostrich position on the seats of the bus so that their naked spread buttocks were pressed against the windows.

The military buttocks loomed at us from the windows of the bus. They looked like huge white one-eyed sea monsters in a tank. The nasty ink black eyes of the anuses stared at us. They were very malevolent and they seemed to be surrounded by murky perimeters that varied in their shades of darkness.

Once the coach had vanished, it was the aggression of this military display rather than its obscenity which seemed foul. The act was frightening because it had been prepared with all the precision of a superb military tactic. The trousers must have all been down as the soldiers passed the police who guarded the gate. The timing of the soldiers had been excellent for it had needed skill to get all those spread buttocks into every window of the coach so that we could be afforded a bird's-eye view of so many anal passages.

It didn't occur to any of us to take the number of the coach. There didn't seem much point. The military had all the power on the perimeter and they could use that power as they wished.

It didn't occur to any of us to complain to the British police who were working for the base. What if they were to say they had seen nothing – that we had suffered a hallucination, that we all longed to see rows of military anuses and we had conjured them up out of wishful thinking? Much the same fears that prevent rape victims reporting the attacks that have been made on them made us asume we would not be believed.

When we joined the women round their camp fire they were oblivious of the little display of military aggression that had just taken place in the lane. We didn't mention it to them. It would only have depressed them. They had to put up with so much sadistic male behaviour on the perimeter that they would have shrugged. Anuses were bared on

Greenham Common. There was nothing much that women could do.

The campers at Main Gate had just received requests from the peace movements in the United States. The Americans were asking to be sent ferns and stones from the Common at Greenham.

Sitting in all the mess and discomfort of the camp at Main Gate where soldiers came out of the missile base with their naked buttocks spreadeagled, it seemed astonishing that Americans could want anything from this odious British Common.

Yet it appeared that it could still provide something precious enough to be considered worthy of souvenirs. The American request for ferns and stones pin-pointed the extra-ordinary ambivalence in the way that the Greenham women were regarded. The same ambivalence that divided the residents of Newbury was represented internationally.

The Greenham women could be seen as such dangerous scum that it was considered justifiable to shower them with any kind of excrement. The shit could be real, like that of the Newbury hooligans, or it could be symbolic like that of the soldiers who defended the Cruise missile.

Then from a totally opposing view, the Greenham women were so admired for their courage and self-sacrifice that they were regarded with the respect accorded to saints. When the American peace movements asked for ferns and stones, they were asking for something similar to holy relics.

After I left Main Gate that day, I went to the Newbury hotel and picked up a travel brochure that was lying around for tourists. It was entitled 'Beautiful Berkshire'.

The text conjured up a 'Royal Berkshire' that I found all the more foreign and imaginary because I'd just been exposed to some of the ugliness of this 'royal county' as it existed round the missile base.

'West Berkshire offers the visitor one of the most colourful and varied areas in southern England. Windswept downs hiding neat villages with their ponds, pubs and racing stables. The green Kennet Valley threaded by the peaceful canal.

Towns like Newbury with its civil war battles, steeped in the history of horse racing. There are woods to walk in and commons to explore ...'

The writer of the brochure was doing his best to make the area sound still attractive. All the colour and variation that he claimed visitors would find in the county was still there, although the visitor might not like all of it as much as the pamphlet for tourists intended.

The pubs, the racing stables were unspoilt, and the green Kennet Valley could still be sweetly described as 'threaded' by a peaceful canal.

The civil war traditions of Newbury were still metaphorically represented in the clash between the Newburians, who were rising to the bugle call of RAGE, and those who let the peace campers take baths in their houses and drove around with signs that said 'Wood for the Greenham Women' displayed on the back of their cars. Within the civil war climate of the town, this was a brave thing to do. It invited some anti-women youth to hurl a brick through their car windows.

It was depressing to read the Newbury pamphlets for tourists. It was a travesty when its writer made the whole area sound so peaceful and innocent. The Cruise missile, which symbolized violence, seemed to be able to stir up violence in the territory that surrounded it. It could spread hatred and dissension just as it could spread plutonium dust.

The writer urged visitors to explore the local commons. What a very uninspiring and melancholy exploration that could now turn out to be. All the visitor was likely to discover, as he searched for wild flowers, gorse, and heather, was small-town cruelty that flowered in the shadow of the concrete silos that harboured one of humanity's greatest current symbols of cruelty. He might also discover a horrifying lack of military discipline amongst the soldiers who had been entrusted to defend one of the most dangerous weapons on earth.

13

When the camp at Main Gate was finally evicted, some of the women set fire to their own benders when they saw the bailiffs coming. The polythene of their dwellings, when ignited, flew up in the air like flaming balloons.

'We felt we were burning the whole mess and the stupidity of the evictions,' one of the women said to me. 'We are never going to leave.'

There were only thirty women camping at Main Gate, but the authorities felt that four hundred police were required to move them, and the peace women were soon pushed and bodily dragged from the scruffy piece of land where they had lived for so many months.

For several miles, the roads surrounding Newbury were sealed off. Officially it was claimed there had been a road accident. The peace women were convinced that this was a legal manoeuvre to prevent them receiving provisions from outside supporters.

The supporters were as stubborn as the Greenham women. Despite the blockades, some of them walked long distances carrying the usual dry wood and polythene and candles.

The bulldozers were brought in to the land outside Main Gate and started churning it up. It was soon a mountain of rubble. The bulldozers smashed down the silver birches and the gorse which was growing near it. The unfortunate Common developed a new kind of eyesore.

There were always certain parallels between the Greenham women and the Greek women in the *Lysistrata*. Both groups of women banded together and rejected men in order to protest the pointlessness of war, the waste of national resources, the murder of their sons. Aristophanes' play was a comedy and he could resolve the male–female conflict light-heartedly. The play that was being enacted on Greenham Common had no such easy resolution, and it had undertones that were not comic.

At Main Gate that day, the army and the law were behaving as if they felt the women had to be crushed because they had seized the Acropolis. The little piece of ruined land round the Main Gate was hardly the Acropolis. When it was grabbed back from the rebel women, very little of value seemed to have been accomplished.

The women moved a few yards away from their old camper's site and they lit a fire. Its illegal smoke showed that they did not see themselves as defeated.

A new wooden fence was erected to prevent them from returning to the land immediately outside the Main Gate. The base now had an extra fence to protect a bit of its perimeter, but whether this was worth all the expense was questionable. Rows of police stood in front of the newly erected fence. All day they guarded it from the peace women. The old lady in the tweed cape would have probably been outraged to see the manpower of so many police devoted to an enterprise that did so little to combat the muggers of Newbury.

As the rows of blue-uniformed men stood hour by hour in front of the patch of land that was being systematically mutilated by the snorting, crashing bulldozers, they had the grim resolution of men who had been chosen to defend their country. The little section of their country that they were guarding was in a pitiful state and they didn't look as if they were very proud of their stalwart position. They had all the power and all the weapons, but as they put up this massive fight against such a small group of pacifist women, all they seemed to lack was the worthy opponent. Once again the Greenham women's protest which only had moral force, if it had any force at all, was being treated as if it needed physical force to quell it.

The press arrived to photograph the defeat of the peace

women. The policewomen who were helping to enforce the evictions became irritable and nervous when photographers tried to take their pictures, whereas the male police tolerated being photographed. The role of the policewomen was a strange one during the evictions and some of them looked very embarrassed and unhappy. The Greenham women saw them as traitors and the policewomen seemed to have a horror of allowing it to be put on permanent historic record that they'd enforced duties which other women saw as a betrayal of their sex.

When the Greenham women were tried for illegal acts and breach of the peace, they maintained that it was the British government that was acting illegally in housing genocidal weapons, that it was contravening the Genocide Act, passed by Parliament in 1969.

When they were sent to Holloway Prison for breaching the peace, they would try to tell the magistrates that the threat of nuclear war was 'breaching their peace'. Sometimes the Newbury magistrates would ask to be spared from any political speeches from the Greenham women. They wanted to get on with the case in hand. They knew they had all the garbled testimony about the wilful damage to the perimeter in front of them, and that was going to be quite exhausting enough. They couldn't always face the prospect of a stream of Greenham women making statements of their general position which would introduce extraneous, even more exhausting legal arguments, and delay the court from making a thorough examination of all the refinements and minutiae of the crime that was under their specific attention.

As the slip-road that led to the Main Gate of the missile base grew wider and wider, the peace women watched the destructive activities of the bulldozers and they recognized that the authorities might feel it was worth spending £150,000 worth of the ratepayers' money in order to make this little road more suitable for the use of the carrier of the warheads as it made its excursions through the British countryside. They also recognized that the authorities might feel it was worth all the expense of maintaining a grotesquely large police presence in order to see that this costly 'widening' was completed without interference from the peace protestors.

But they were also aware that there was another reason why their opponents felt this outlay of public money was well spent. While the Greenham women remained at the gates of the base, they continually 'breached the peace' of the British public. Their presence there was a continual reminder that the nuclear and military experts could make errors, that military, scientific, and political experts had made catastrophic errors in the past. The Greenham women also knew that they 'breached the peace' of the British government as they reminded the nation of the vast sums of money that were being spent on maintaining these weapons while British health and education services were allowed to deteriorate with every passing week.

The peace women called out 'shame' to the drivers of the bulldozers as they drove their great machines into the silver birches and the gorse. One of the drivers got so rattled by their disapproval that he not only mowed down the trees and the gorse, but he suddenly lost his head and he seemed unable to stop there. For no reason that was obvious to the spectator, he suddenly drove his machine right through the brand-new expensive fence that had only that morning been erected to protect the perimeter from the protestors.

The women laughed as they watched his inept performance. He went scarlet. His position could hardly have been more embarrassing. He'd seriously damaged a government fence, not wilfully, but out of some kind of nervous hysteria which had made him mismanage his enormous machine. He had committed this act of destruction while watched by women who desperately disapproved of the way he was ripping up the Common and the reasons why he was doing it. Symbolically, he had destroyed the defences of those whose side he was working on.

By his clumsy bulldozing action, this driver had given the most unexpected demonstration of the good reasons for the mistrust of the male handling of instruments of power that had brought the women to camp on the missile base.

'I wonder if that fellow rather hates what he's paid to do,' one of the women said. 'It's really odd that he's just made things easier for us rather than the military!' She shrugged and made a French toast on the fire of the women's new camp. 'No, I don't expect he hates what he's doing. He probably doesn't think about it. He's probably like most of the men who work inside the base.'

The police, who were guarding the new fence, had to bring in workmen to repair what the driver had done to it. An unbelievable number of police vans kept drawing up at Main Gate as if reinforcements were needed to quell a dangerous and bloody revolt.

The women made tea in their new camp and they did what they had always done – they just sat around. They obviously had no intention of leaving. They claimed that for every five women who were evicted, fifteen more joined the camps in order to protest.

A British ex-magistrate looked at all the hordes of police with a shudder. She had been sent to jail many times since she had become a Greenham woman. 'I wonder if this country can continue to have nuclear weapons without turning into a police state,' she said. 'More people ought to ask that. Who cares whether it's wrong to be lesbian and all that trivial, frivolous nonsense? All that's always only used to camouflage the issues that really matter.'

As I hung about Main Gate on the day of the peace women's most important symbolic day of eviction, their peace movement seemed just about as powerful as the pieces of wool with which they darned the perimeter. They believed that by their presence on Greenham Common they were acting as symbolic candles that represented the conscience of humanity.

Looking at the absurdly large police presence that had been gathered round the wire of the base to crush them, such candles appeared all too easy to snuff out. I couldn't tell if the Greenham women had been defeated. Their camp had certainly been driven a little further from the Main Gate of the missile base. That was not an important defeat. Their position had always been ideological rather than merely geographic.

Even if they were driven very much further from the perimeter, they would continue to give their terrifying warning. The great powers might defeat their protest – but the glorious victory could only be pyrrhic.

Afterword

The peace women at Greenham Common are now battling through their fourth terrible winter as they continue their protest on the site of the Cruise Missile.

Mrs Thatcher's first act on returning from her vacation this summer was to renew her pledge to the nation that she would get rid of the Greenham women. It was as if she felt that of all the very serious problems with which Great Britain is currently confronted, the destruction of the peace camps was the one the most urgently deserving of her attention.

Yet despite the solemn pledge of the Prime Minister, the Greenham women are still defiantly there. Their message remains the same. 'Don't leave it to someone else. There is no one else.'

Four years ago a small group of women and children walked three hundred miles from Wales to protest the illegal housing of a genocidal weapon. The British parliament passed the genocide act soon after the last war and it was declared illegal to manufacture or house weapons that are capable of mass extermination. This act was never repealed, but the British government has conveniently decided to forget it. The women vowed that they would not leave the perimeter fence that encircles the Cruise Missile while their government persisted in flouting the law. At the time it was not generally imagined that they would be able to keep up their protest for very long. It seemed most unlikely that they would survive one single winter. Now they have survived three and have just got through their fourth hellish Christmas.

Just as certain viruses when over-exposed to antibiotics develop a resistance and become immune, so Mrs Thatcher's government seems to have developed an amazing strain of courageous women who seem immune to hardship, persecution, and humiliation.

The police treat them with ever-increasing savagery, and when they make their arrests they now seize the women by their breasts in order to make the whole procedure as degrading and painful as possible. At night, when the women are zipped up and trying to sleep in their survival bags, the police pick them up as if they are bags of garbage and hurl them down on the ground so that they get very badly bruised. When they come round in order to extinguish the camp fires with hydrants, they also squirt the women so that they are left fireless in the snow with all their clothing drenched. 'They even squirt the poor camp cat,' a woman told me. 'I think that is really disgusting.'

Yet the women go on with their protest. The septic tanks they once used as toilets have been destroyed. The only tap that had any water in the camps has been cut off. Bulldozers come round three times a day and plough up the ground where the women are camping, turning it into great black swimming pools of icy water. A homemade bomb was recently exploded only a few yards from where the protestors were trying to sleep. Yet while they stoically put up with all this harassment, the media continues to criticise them for dressing badly.

The peace movement in Ulster was smeared and discredited by the accusation that the peace women were wearing fur coats. Now the protestors at Greenham Common are discredited for *not* wearing fur coats. There is something ludicrous in the demand for high fashion in the subhuman conditions of the camps beside the Cruise Missile. Wading around in deep, freezing mud and snow like soldiers in the trenches of the First World War, if the women were to wear the flowing chiffon and the sables their critics appear to demand, it would be inappropriate to the point of lunacy.

The women take the criticisms of their clothes with a shrug but they are sensitive to the charge that they are 'bad' mothers. They feel that if a man leaves his family and goes off to fight for a cause that he believes in he is regarded as a hero, whereas if a woman does the same thing she is regarded as irresponsible and heartless. Their detractors ask what they have achieved after so much self-sacrifice. They have prevented the whole question of the sanity of current international nuclear policies from being forgotten and brushed away from public consciousness. Thousands and thousands of women have gone to visit Greenham Common from all over the world. It has become a place of pilgrimage. Thousands of American women have gone there and have spent weeks living in the camps. The support that the camps receive from the United States is enormous. Innumerable survivor-victims from Hiroshima and Nagasaki have visited Greenham Common and they say that the very existence of this protest gives them a tiny bit of hope. These Japanese survivors have found it horrifying and astonishing when members of RAGE have approached them and tried to get their sympathy because the Greenham women have made use of the public baths in Newbury.

Even from countries as remote as New Zealand, Maori women have sent delegations to Greenham Common. Soviet women have staged eight peaceful demonstrations in front of the British Embassy in Moscow and have been jailed for protesting the arrests of the Greenham women.

Last February the Greenham women failed for the third time in their attempt to sue Ronald Reagan and Casper Weinberger in a New York court. They never hoped to win the case, but they wanted the evidence they could produce to be heard. They were trying to sue the American leaders for illegal deployment of genocidal weapons; and Robert Aldridge, one of the chief designers of the nuclear missiles at Lockheed, was prepared to testify on their behalf. So was Admiral Gene La Rocque, who has resigned from the US Navy in order to protest the illegality of manufacturing and deploying First Strike weapons. Their case was dismissed on the same grounds that were used against plaintiffs who protested the illegality of the Vietnam war.

The Judge deemed the issues too complicated to be 'manageable by judicial standards.'

Auden said of Freud that he was not a man, he was a climate, and in the same sense the Greenham women are an international moral climate.

They have now broken into the control tower of the base so many times that they know their way around this huge military installation much better than any of the American and British paratroupers who defend it. The regiments come and go, but the women remain.

There is another irony in the situation at Greenham. If Mrs Thatcher carries out her pledge and drives the women from the site of the Cruise Missile she will be doing herself a disservice. It would be very difficult for any terrorist to enter the base while the women are there keeping their sleepless, stubborn vigil in the mud. The military are obviously incapable of defending the Cruise Missile, otherwise the women would not be able to make their nightly visits to the control tower. They go into the base with the same regularity with which housewives visit the supermarket. It is curious that the Greenham women have got into a position in which they have become guardians of the dreaded warheads when they are only trying to do the best they can to guard the shaky future of the planet.

—LONDON, MARCH 1985